LITERARY/CULTURAL THEORY

DALIT LITERATURE AND CRITICISM

Literary/Cultural Theory provides concise and lucid introductions to a range of key concepts and theorists in contemporary literary and cultural theory. Original and contemporary in presentation, and eschewing jargon, each book in the series presents students of humanities and social sciences exhaustive overviews of theories and theorists, while also introducing them to the mechanics of reading literary/cultural texts using critical tools. Each book also carries glossaries of key terms and ideas, and pointers for further reading and research. Written by scholar-teachers who have taught critical theory for years, and vetted by some of the foremost experts in the field, the series Literary/Cultural Theory is indispensable to students and teachers.

Also in the series

Feminisms
Psychoanalytic Theory and Criticism
Jacques Lacan
Subaltern Studies
Ecocriticism
Postcolonialism Now
Marxist Literary and Cultural Theory
Postsecular Theory
Nations and Nationalisms
Periyar
Popular Culture
Queer Studies
Frantz Fanon
Mikhail Bakhtin
Deconstruction and Poststructuralism
Edward Said
Diaspora Theory and Transnationalism
Life Writing

LITERARY/CULTURAL THEORY

DALIT LITERATURE AND CRITICISM

RAJ KUMAR
University of Delhi

Orient BlackSwan

DALIT LITERATURE AND CRITICISM

ORIENT BLACKSWAN PRIVATE LIMITED

Registered Office
3-6-752 Himayatnagar, Hyderabad 500 029, Telangana, India
Email: centraloffice@orientblackswan.com

Other Offices
Bengaluru, Chennai, Guwahati, Hyderabad, Kolkata,
Mumbai, New Delhi, Noida, Patna

First published 2019
Reprinted 2022 (twice), 2024

ISBN 978 93 5287 532 0

Typeset in Aldine 401 BT 10.5/13 *by*
Akhil Offset Printers
Hyderabad 500 020

Printed at
B.B. Press
Tronica City Ghaziabad (UP) 201102

Published by
Orient Blackswan Private Limited
3-6-753, Himayatnagar,
Hyderabad 500 029, Telangana, India
Email: info@orientblackswan.com

Contents

Contents

Preface

Dalit Literature and Criticism is an attempt to write and develop a critical literary history and theory of Dalit literature. Modern Dalit literature is already more than five decades old, if we take its foundation to be the establishment of the Dalit Panthers in 1972 in Maharashtra. Today Dalit literature is available in every Indian language. During this period, Dalit writers have shown that Dalit literature is worth reading for its new aesthetic values. Dalit literature has also had a considerable impact on the Indian literary scene. It is now seriously read, discussed, translated, interpreted and critiqued by general readers as well as academics. Scholars belonging to various disciplines – sociology, history, economics, philosophy, psychology, law and political science, apart from language and literature – have started using Dalit literature for the purposes of teaching and research. Dalit literature is, thus, studied across disciplines with the help of existing traditional literary theories. But a cursory glance of any Dalit text will reveal that traditional literary theories, however radical they may be, will not be able to do justice to the kind of reading Dalit literature demands. Dalit literature is the creative expression of a people who were silent for a long time. A scholar of Dalit literature has to address a number of issues when approaching this vast and varied body of writing. What do they write? Which language do they use? Whom do they address? How do we understand their writing? We could say that Dalit writings are both stories and histories of Dalit communities which reflect a radicalisation in Dalit lives. Dalit creative expressions, therefore, need to be understood in the context of the sociological, historical and political aspects of Dalit lifeworlds. The present book is a modest attempt in that direction.

The book is written for both researchers and general readers, as an attempt to introduce them to Dalit literature and various critical practices. Using simple language, the book seeks to provide a survey of important theoretical as well as pedagogical concepts relating to Dalit literature. Apart from literary criticism, the book also introduces several cultural concepts relating to Dalit lives.

Keeping this background in mind, the book has been divided into the following chapters. The first chapter introduces the concept of 'Dalit' in a comprehensive way. Since the word 'Dalit' is an outcome of Indian caste society, the chapter traces its various meanings over phases of Indian history. The second chapter situates Dalit lives in the context of caste. Tracing the anti-caste intellectual history beginning from the Lokayata or Charvaka movement, the chapter maps out the way Jainism, Buddhism, Bhakti saint–poets, and later, non-brahmin leaders such as Jotiba Phule, B. R. Ambedkar, Periyar and others vehemently fought against discriminatory caste practices. The third chapter studies the background to the emergence of Dalit literature. Tracing the historical origin of the formation of the Dalit Panthers Movement of 1972 in Maharashtra, the chapter also deals with the way Dalit writers and activists worked with social and political commitment towards the growth of Dalit literature. The fourth chapter has been devoted to bringing out the various theoretical and philosophical debates around Dalit literature and aesthetics. Issues such as Dalit genre, Dalit aesthetics, Dalit language, Dalit imagination, Dalit myths and other such theoretical frameworks have been elaborated upon, taking different viewpoints offered by both theorists and authors into consideration. The fifth chapter is about Dalit literary criticism in practice. Akhila Naik's novel *Bheda* (2010), which has the distinction of being the first Odia Dalit novel, has been critically analysed in this chapter. The sixth chapter deals with pedagogical approaches to Dalit literature: Dalit studies, like English studies or gender studies, has now become established in many universities in India and abroad. The concluding chapter summarises the arguments and looks forward to new ways of reading Dalit literature across languages and cultures. The book also has a comprehensive bibliography followed by a list of texts for further reading. At the end of the book a glossary of important terms has been provided for easy comprehension of the text.

Several people have helped me in the preparation of this book. I am thankful to one and all. It was Sreenath Sreedharan from Orient

BlackSwan who made the proposal of writing this book. While I accepted his proposal, I could not meet the deadline due to my other commitments. I want to thank Sreenath for his persuasiveness and patience and for having faith in me. I am equally thankful to Namrata Kartik from Orient BlackSwan whose meticulous editing has made significant improvements to the book. I am also indebted to Rohan Kamble, Swarnima Bhattacharya, Himanshi Sharma, Tanu Sharma, Animesh Mohapatra, Aruni Mahapatra, Aratrika Das, Lalit Kumar, Gautam Choube, Nandini Chandra, Ira Raja and Hany Babu who read parts of my chapters and offered their suggestions within a short period of time. I am really thankful to them. I also want to acknowledge my sincere thanks to my MPhil students whose interventions during discussions both inside and outside classrooms have shaped many of the arguments made in this book. Last, but not the least, I will never forget the loving care I continue to receive from my daughter, Ishita, and my wife, Bedamati. When I neglected them while writing this book, they supported me wholeheartedly. In my absence it was Bedamati who looked after the family needs. As my humble thanks, I offer this book to her.

Chapter One

Introducing the Concept of 'Dalit'

Broadly speaking, the word 'Dalit' is a political term which symbolises the relatively new identity of a group of people who were earlier known as 'untouchables'. Untouchability is a deeply ingrained consequence of the caste system and is an unacceptable and hurtful social practice. It was abolished when the Indian Constitution came into effect in 1950. In spite of its legal abolition, untouchability continues to be practised in different forms and degrees in almost all parts of India even today. Thus, the term 'Dalit' clearly suggests that caste as a social system is still prevalent in India. Dalits are struggling hard to reclaim their human dignity and self-respect. The rise of Dalit movements and Dalit literature is an example of how Dalits have become a new political community. Through their writings and activities they have been speaking truth to power.

Dalit lives have almost always been circumscribed by rigid caste rules. Apart from being 'untouchable', they were also 'un-seeable', 'unapproachable' and 'un-hearable' by most castes. They were considered as the lowest of the low and treated worse than animals by Hindus, Muslims, Christians, Sikhs, Buddhists, Parsis, and other religious communities. Their rights and liberties were curtailed under pernicious caste rules. Their caste status meant that they remained illiterate, poor and downtrodden through most of Indian history. It is only after independence that they were able to avail of modern education (something that is still a struggle) and became speaking subjects asserting their rights and freedom. Thus the term 'Dalit' has an intrinsic relationship with the nature and character of Indian caste society. To understand its meaning, we have to study the intricately interwoven notions of caste in society that have evolved over the centuries in India.

LOCATING DALITS

The caste system (as found in India) is generally believed to be unique to Indian society. As a social hierarchy, it divides the entire Hindu population into two categories: upper castes and lower castes. This social division is permanent, and is backed by a number of Hindu religious scriptures collectively known as Dharma shastras. There are as many as 220 Dharma shastras written in Sanskrit, which is one of the classical languages much revered by Hindus. The Dharma shastras are basically law books composed by brahmins to enforce caste rules mostly among Dalits, lower castes and women. Since the basic principle of the caste system is to uphold social divisions based on what the sociologists term as 'purity' and 'pollution' concepts, these Hindu law books are codes of conduct written especially to administer religious sanctions to the lower castes, especially Dalits. These sanctions generally helped the caste system to renew its legitimacy even after it was legally challenged. As a result, the caste system, with its myriad variations and complexities, is able to persist in all regions of India even today with different degrees of rigidity.

Dalits constitute about sixteen per cent of the country's population, numbering more than 220 million and spread all over India. Apart from India, Dalits are also native to other parts of South Asia, such as, Pakistan, Bangladesh, Nepal, Sri Lanka and Myanmar. As a diaspora community they can be found in the United States, United Kingdom, Singapore, Malaysia, South Africa, Canada and the Caribbean. Variously known as ati-shudras, chandalas, panchamas, antyajas, achhuts, asprushyas, Depressed Classes, harijans and the Scheduled Castes in different periods in Indian history, Dalits still suffer the stigma of untouchability even after caste discrimination has been declared an offence under Article 17 of the Indian Constitution. They are socially frail, economically needy and politically powerless. Even though a small section of Dalits have prospered under government patronage – thanks to reservation policies in education, employment and politics – and have moved up economically and professionally, socially they remain unaccepted. It does not seem to matter that Dalits are politically and economically the equals of anyone in free India. When they try to rise up the social scale, they are very often brutally crushed by the upper castes and sometimes by the state machinery. Their oppressors resort to mob-raids, murder, arson and rape.

Dalits, however, are now conscious of their rights to live with dignity and self-respect and, therefore, have been interrogating and challenging the hegemony of upper castes and classes. This has clearly been reflected in the recent emergence of Dalit literature, which is a part of the Dalit liberation movement. Before we discuss the various aspects of either the Dalit liberation movement or Dalit literature, it would be useful to understand the origin of the term 'Dalit'. What does the term 'Dalit' signify? What exactly is its meaning? What was the point of its origin? Who really coined it? What is its context? The present chapter will make an attempt to answer these questions.

DEFINING AND REDEFINING THE TERM 'DALIT'

The etymology of the term 'Dalit' can be traced to the root word *dal* in Sanskrit, which means to crack, split, be broken or torn asunder, trodden down, scattered, crushed, destroyed, and is understood in all the Indian languages that are derived from Sanskrit. As a noun and adjective, 'Dalit' can be used for all genders: masculine, feminine and neuter. In the words of A. P. Nirmal, who pioneered Dalit theology in India, 'the Dalits are 1) the broken, the torn, the rent, the burst, the split; 2) the opened, the expanded; 3) the bisected; 4) the driven asunder, the dispelled, the scattered; 5) the downtrodden, the crushed, the destroyed; and 6) the manifested, the displayed' (139).

Even though the term 'Dalit' can be understood in all Indian languages, its academic use was not very common across states in the past. Maharashtra is known to have pioneered the Dalit movement and Dalit literature, and Marathi was, perhaps, the first Indian language to have recorded the frequent use of the term in the public sphere beginning from the early part of the nineteenth century. For example, the Marathi version of the term 'Dalit' was first found in Molesworth's Marathi–English dictionary's 1831 edition, which was later reprinted in 1975. The dictionary gives the meaning of the term 'Dalit' as 'ground, broken or reduced to pieces generally' suggesting all kinds of disabilities – be it social, economic, political or cultural (qtd. in Zelliot 267). Thus the various meanings of the term clearly delineate all the characteristics of caste hierarchies which subjugate Dalits, women and lower castes to the utmost. If such is the case, one wonders, how the term came to be used in Indian society and literature across language and culture? Let us try to understand the various meanings of the term and their implications.

Going by available sources, it can be said that the term 'Dalit' came to be used in public discourse towards the end of the nineteenth century. It was Jotibarao Phule (1826–90), one of the pioneers of the non-brahmin movement in Maharashtra, who was supposed to have used the term 'Dalit' to describe the condition of the outcastes and untouchables as oppressed and exploited people who were maltreated by the upper castes. Phule especially blamed two upper-caste communities, the baniyas and brahmins, whom he termed as 'Sethji-Bhatji', for this caste exploitation. He called for the shudras and ati-shudras to come together and fight against what he called 'caste slavery'. Phule's deliberate use of the term 'Dalit', already in use in colloquial Marathi, initiated a public discourse against the menace of brahminism throughout the nineteenth century.

Later, B. R. Ambedkar (1891–1956), the architect of the Indian Constitution and the tallest Dalit leader of the Dalit movement so far, used this term particularly in his Marathi speeches and occasionally in his Marathi writings, along with the other terms, such as 'bahishkrut' and 'asprushya varga'. Ambedkar considered Phule one of his gurus, the other two being Buddha and Kabir. Having been heavily influenced by the revolutionary ideas of these reformers who fiercely fought against the caste system in their own time, Ambedkar took the caste fight one step further by making it a national issue and dedicated his entire life to fighting against it (the details of which will be discussed in the next chapter). As an anti-caste intellectual, Ambedkar deeply studied the Vedas, Vedanta and the Dharma shastras and rejected the claims made by brahmins that the caste system was divinely sanctified by the gods. Instead, he offered new interpretations of these Hindu texts based on historical evidence. For example, in his famous book *The Untouchables: Who Were They and Why They Became Untouchables?* (1948), he states that the untouchables at one point of time belonged to kshatriya communities. Since they carried out menial and manual work, they were looked down upon by the brahmins, and were relegated to the margins and became the untouchables. Certain strictures were imposed upon them, some of which could have resulted in their consumption of beef, which was seen as an act of sacrilege according to the brahmins. Their rejection of the oppressive caste structure of Hinduism and embracing of Buddhism sealed their status as outsiders. Studying the socioeconomic conditions of untouchables in ancient times, Ambedkar coined the term 'the Broken Men', indicating that the forefathers of the Dalits were forced to live humiliating lives under the caste system. Thus, Ambedkar's life-long struggle was to fight against caste to build an egalitarian Indian society. But for Dalits, the annihilation of caste has remained a distant dream. Caste atrocities continue to be perpetuated against them, and the upper castes are still intolerant of Dalit subjectivity.

With the rise of Dalit movements across states and the emergence of Dalit literature, Dalits started to become speaking subjects. They became more and more organised and came together to demand their rightful place in Indian society. An early example of this was seen in Maharashtra when Dalit activists and writers came together in 1972 to launch a united Dalit movement famously known as the Dalit Panther movement. J. V. Pawar, Namdeo Dhasal and Raja Dhale were the founder-members of the Dalit Panthers. With the formation of Dalit Panthers the term 'Dalit' became commonly used in the public sphere, first in Maharashtra and later all over India.

The manifesto of the Dalit Panthers defined the term 'Dalit' in an inclusive manner. It says 'Dalits' are those who are 'members of Scheduled Castes and Tribes, neo-Buddhists, the working people, the landless and the poor peasants, women and all those who are being exploited politically, economically and in the name of religion' (qtd. in Joshi 145). The definition given by the Panthers encompasses caste, class, ethnicity, gender and minority communities across religions who are naturally opposed to Hindu upper caste/class men. The Dalit Panthers gave a detailed explanation for using the term 'Dalit' in such a historical context:

> We must pay attention to the objective process of social development and make an historical analysis of the power that imprisons the Dalit and which has succeeded in making him tie his own hands. The Hindu feudal rule can be a hundred times more ruthless today in oppressing the Dalits than it was in the Muslim period or the British period. Because the Hindu feudal rule has in its hand all the arteries of production, bureaucracy, judiciary, army and police forces, in the shape of feudal landlords, capitalists and religious leaders who stand behind and enable these instruments to strive. Hence, the problem of untouchability of the Dalits is no more of mere mental slavery. Untouchability is the most violent form of exploitation on the face of earth, which survives the ever-changing forms of the power structure. Today, it is necessary to seek its soil, its root causes. If we understand them, we can definitely strike at the heart of its exploitation. . . . Truly speaking, the problem of the Dalits or Scheduled Castes and Tribes, have become a broad problem; the Dalit is no longer merely an untouchable outside the village walls and the Scripture. He is untouchable and he is a Dalit, but he is also a worker, a landless labourer, a proletarian. (Joshi 141–42)

In their manifesto, the Panthers emphasise that the structures of Indian society are based on caste, whereby caste and power go hand in hand. Accordingly, work in India is distributed along caste lines. The upper castes in India are privileged enough to not do any physical work. Hence, they consider themselves 'high' castes. Shudras and Dalits, on the other hand, are responsible for all kinds of menial and manual work which, according to the caste system, are considered to be 'low'. In spite of being 'low' in social standing, shudras are 'touchable' and hence acceptable in Indian caste society. On the other hand, Dalits are not only placed at the bottom of the caste hierarchy, but are branded as 'untouchable', and therefore they are 'unacceptable' to caste society. They are forced to do all kinds of menial jobs which involve physical stamina, fierce courage and perseverance. It is in this context that Dalits can also be seen as workers, landless labourers, and the proletariat in Indian caste society.

What was the reason for the Panthers to use such a unique term? Indian caste society, over the years, has used several names to describe the people of untouchable communities, such as ati-shudra, Exterior Castes, outcaste, Depressed Classes, harijan, Scheduled Castes, ex-untouchables, and so on. Dalits felt that these terms coined by upper-caste Hindus, officials, social reformers and others were abusive in nature and synonymous with derogation, domination and paternalism. That is why the people belonging to this category preferred to describe themselves as Dalits which includes all forms of oppression, be it caste, class, ethnicity, language, religion or gender. Eleanor Zelliot, an American scholar who has done extensive research on Ambedkar's movement in Maharashtra as early as 1976, writes,

> In the early 1970s two Maharashtrian movements achieved enough prominence to be noticed by the English language press, the Dalit Panthers and Dalit literature. By substituting the word "Black" for "Dalit" the reader can immediately understand that a phenomenon comparable to the American Black Panthers and Black literature has surfaced among the lower caste in social and literary affairs in Western India. Like the American movements, the Dalit Panthers and the Dalit School of literature represent a new level of pride, militancy and sophisticated creativity. The Marathi word "Dalit", like the word Black, was chosen by the group itself. . . . Dalit implies those who have been broken, ground down by those above them in a deliberate and active way. There is in the word itself an inherent denial of pollution, Karma, and justified caste hierarchy. (267)

The Dalit Panthers, by using the term 'Dalit', were systematically rejecting all caste-related positions the former untouchables were known for in Indian society. By rejecting their caste positions, they were also asserting a new kind of identity which would give them self-pride and dignity. Ever since the Dalit Panthers coined the term 'Dalit', its connotation has been changing. The term is evolving and has acquired new meanings across academic boundaries. For example, Namdeo Dhasal, the well-known Marathi poet and one of the leaders of the Dalit Panthers movement, infused the term with a leftist vision to include not just the Scheduled Castes but also economically oppressed classes, including the Scheduled Tribes, neo-Buddhists, landless labourers, and all those who are economically exploited. Dhasal was heavily influenced by Marxist ideologies and he defined the term 'Dalit' in terms of class, generally including women, tribals, workers in industries and agricultural workers, along with the untouchable communities.

For Gangadhar Pantawane, a Dalit activist from Maharashtra who was also the founding editor of *Asmitadarsha* (Mirror of Identity), the chief organ for the spread of Dalit literature in the 1970s, the term 'Dalit' does not refer to a caste, but is a symbol of change and revolution. He defines 'Dalit' in a broader way, saying, 'the Dalit believes in humanism. He rejects the existence of God, rebirth, soul, sacred books that teach discrimination, fate and heaven because these have made him a slave. He represents the exploited men . . .' (Joshi 79). Pantawane, thus, expands the meaning of the term across borders and boundaries to include all oppressed people who are fighting for their equality and freedom.

The references cited above are only a few instances of how the concept 'Dalit' has been interpreted by some Dalit scholars keeping in mind the rubrics of caste, class, ethnicity and gender. A recent addition to these categories is religion, which encompasses all the concepts mentioned above. Therefore, in the public sphere we now frequently hear the terms 'Dalit Muslims', 'Dalit Christians', 'Dalit Sikhs' and 'Dalit Buddhists', which give new meanings to the term 'Dalit'. Since conversion seemed to be a way out of caste structures for the lower castes, they have changed their religion from Hinduism to Islam, Christianity, Sikhism or Buddhism. The irony is that their caste positions still persist even after the change of religion. Hence, terms such as 'Dalit Muslims', 'Dalit Christians', 'Dalit Sikhs' and 'Dalit Buddhists' have come into use. To break this monopoly of caste across religions, social and political activists are working hard to bring about a collective consciousness, which has been termed 'Dalitbahujan' by Kancha Ilaiah. This Dalitbahujan collective has been seeking a greater unity among various oppressed communities such as the Scheduled Castes, the Scheduled Tribes, Other Backward Classes and religious minorities to fight against caste practices prevalent in religious institutions in India. Ilaiah believes that this kind of unity among oppressed communities will bring about social revolution which will give birth to a new social order. In this new social order, as Ilaiah believes, the oppressed Dalitbahujan majority will be able to exercise the power which has been denied to them by the Hindu upper-caste minority over millennia. Ilaiah terms this exercise as 'Dalitization' in his famous book *Why I am Not a Hindu.* He emphasises the liberation of the masses in India:

> The future is that of Dalitbahujans in India. In order to dalitize society, the Dalitbahujan leadership must know its strengths and weaknesses. The Dalitbahujans of India have suffered hardships all through history. Modern democratic socialist revolutions have now given them some scope to liberate themselves. It is only through their liberation that the rest of the society, namely, the "upper" castes, can be liberated. But this process can be very painful and tortuous. (127)

The process Ilaiah talks about is the transfer of power from upper-caste hands to the Dalitbahujans. This process is not as simple as it seems and Iliah acknowledges the difficulties behind it. When Dalits demand their due rights, the upper castes frequently use violent methods, including murder, rape and arson, in order to silence the rising voices of Dalits. These methods of silencing Dalits, of course, are not new. Indian history has witnessed all kinds of methods the upper castes have used in order to prevent Dalits from closing in on the power-centre and occupying key socioeconomic positions. The most prevalent method was and continues to be the stigmatisation of the Dalit body as being polluted or unclean. Gopal Guru, a Dalit theoretician and an eminent social scientist, talks about how the Dalit corporeal body becomes a regular victim of caste-based humiliation. Giving instances from the everyday life of Dalits in India he observes,

> The top of the twice born have created in Dalits a social leper or walking carrion which is sociologically dangerous and hence needs to be physically quarantined. The ideology of purity-pollution helped the top of the twice born to transmute the human body as an aesthetic idea into a "filthy reality". Untouchables are forced to eat human excreta. This atrocious act seeks to reduce the Dalits to the levels of dogs, pigs, and cows that are considered wretched as these animals (not the pampered pets) also eat human excreta. The body of the Dalits is treated as if it is trapped into a septic tank even if it is a vibrant think tank. This is obnoxiously special to the Indian form of reduction. (213)

In order to counter such a caste project, Guru calls for the total rejection of caste which he terms as a 'rejection of rejection'. This rejection of caste is possible only when Dalits start articulating themselves and assert the Dalit subject. The rise of Dalit literature is an example of how Dalit subjectivity has been consciously rejecting various caste stigmas attached to Dalit communities.

Guru's emphasis on Dalit subjectivity can be seen in the articulation of many Dalit writers and activists. One such writer is Sharankumar Limbale. In *Towards an Aesthetic of Dalit Literature: History, Controversies and Considerations*, Limbale underlines the importance of rejecting the inhuman caste system by revolting against it. He suggests that this rejection is 'aimed at the unequal order which has exploited Dalits' (31) all these years. By rejecting an unequal social order, there simultaneously arises the demand for equality, liberty, fraternity and justice by the Dalit communities. This revolt is also a follow-up to the rejection project which is based on Dalit consciousness. This Dalit consciousness has been born out of centuries of Dalit anguish. Limbale describes it as being 'like a flood, with its aggressive character and an insolent, rebellious attitude' (31). Dalit creativity, therefore, is a cry for freedom of a group of people who were earlier denied the right to articulate their voices. Dalit literature is, therefore, a literature of dignity.

In recent times this rebellion has taken a new form. Some Dalit writers and activists have started using their community surnames, previously meant to humiliate and segregate them from other castes, in order to contest caste hegemonies. For example, in West

Bengal the poet-activist Kalyani Thakur has added 'Charal' to her surname indicating that she is proud of being chandal, one of the untouchable communities referred to in the *Manusmriti*. Similarly, the famous Bengali Dalit writer Manoranjan Byapari has published his autobiography titled *Itibritte chandal jibon* (2014; translated as *Interrogating My Chandal Life: An Autobiography of a Dalit* in 2018). A Dalit activist-historian from Uttar Pradesh, Bikram Harijan, who teaches history at the Banaras Hindu University, deliberately uses Gandhi's euphemism 'harijan' in order comment on the fact that a 'bastard' child of India, who, in Hindu parlance is also a god's child, cannot choose either a name or surname without following caste rules. These are a few examples of Dalit assertion which challenge the dominant caste ideology and its influence on the Dalit population. This leads Anand Teltumbde, an eminent Dalit academic, to observe:

> "Dalit", thus, is a political term, a quasi-class identity, devised during the Ambedkarite movement, distinct from the demeaning "Untouchable", and from the inert administrative labels "Depressed Classes", "Scheduled Castes", and certainly from Gandhi's patronizing "Harijans". The term "Dalit" reflected Ambedkar's aspiration that all the Untouchable castes would wear this new identity and form a formidable "Dalit" constituency. Therefore, it was adopted by all Ambedkarite Dalits, initially the Mahars in Maharashtra and slowly thereafter by *the most populous and dominant Dalit castes in other states* (e.g., the Chamars in UP and Punjab, the Malas in Andhra and the Paraiyars in Tamil Nadu) that identified with the Mahars as their equivalent caste. Even after becoming a dominant term, used everywhere, including by the media, and despite its progenitor, Dr Ambedkar, becoming *the* unchallenged Dalit icon, many other Dalit castes have been reluctant to identify with the term or to use it for themselves. The term "Dalit", as such, does not reflect social realities. It reflects caste-based identities which continue to remain the fundamental identities of people. Paradoxically, even though, over the years, "Dalit" became a dominant term of self-reference, lately there has been resurgence in the self-referential use of specific caste names for Dalit castes, to the extent that the future of the term

> "Dalit" now appears uncertain. (Emphasis in the original, Anandhi and Kapadia 54–55)

The concerns Teltumbde raises in the above paragraph are real. After more than seventy years of independence, Dalits are not fully literate. Naturally, illiterate and poor Dalits from rural India have no choice but to fall back upon their upper-caste masters for their day-to-day livelihood. Secondly, government apathy towards Dalits is quite visible. Parties in power employ political rhetoric, stridently calling for the all-round development of Dalits. But in reality, the government is often anti-Dalit. In order to garner votes, the government is often seen playing the Dalit card by dividing the Dalit population into many binaries: rural–urban, literate–illiterate, rich–poor, male–female, Hindu–non-Hindu, and so on. Dalit leadership has to negotiate this multiplicity of differences within Dalit constituencies before attempting to bring them together. Therefore, Dalit movements have, time and again, not succeeded in gaining the necessary momentum to annihilate caste.

CONCLUSION

The term 'Dalit' refers to the existential conditions of a group of people who were earlier known as 'untouchables'. These marginalised peoples are a product of the Hindu caste system. Following caste rules, the untouchables were subjected to all forms of oppression – be it social, political, economic, cultural or religious. The term 'Dalit', therefore, is an act of rebellion used by the former 'untouchables' to acquire a new identity, which stands for pride and self-respect. Jotibarao Phule and B. R. Ambedkar were the early anti-caste intellectuals who used the term 'Dalit' in their public speeches. Later, the Dalit Panthers of Maharashtra popularised the term through their writings. The emergence of Dalit literature gave a new dimension to the rising consciousness of Dalit subjectivity. Before examining the various aspects and shape of Dalit literature, let us try and address a few questions relating to the Dalit experience of caste as this is what provides the emotional and physical landscape against which Dalit literature emerged. What were the reasons for Dalits to be oppressed in the Indian caste society? Who devised plans to oppress them? Were there any protests against caste exploitation? What was the nature of such protests? These and many other questions will be addressed in the next chapter.

REFERENCES

Ambedkar, B. R. *The Untouchables: Who Were They and Why They Became Untouchables*. Bombay: The Education Department, Government of Maharashtra, 1990. Print.

Anandhi, S. and Kapadia, Karin, eds. *Dalit Women: Vanguard of an Alternative Politics in India*. London: Routledge, 2017. Print

Dangle, Arjun, ed. *Poisoned Bread: Translations from Modern Marathi Dalit Literature*. Bombay: Orient Longman, 1992. Print.

Guru, Gopal, ed. *Humiliation: Claims and Context*. New Delhi: Oxford UP, 2009. Print.

Ilaiah, Kancha. *Why I am Not a Hindu: A Sudra Critique of Hindutva Philosophy, Culture and Political Economy*. Calcutta: Samya, 1996. Print.

Joshi, Barbara, ed. *Untouchable: Voices of the Dalit Liberation Movement*. New Delhi: Select Book Service Syndicate, 1986. Print.

Limbale, Sharankumar. *Towards an Aesthetic of Dalit Literature: History, Controversies and Cosiderations*. Trans. Alok Mukherjee. New Delhi: Orient Longman, 2004. Print.

Nirmal, Arvind P. *Heuristic Explorations*. Madras: CLS, 1990. Print.

Zelliot, Eleanor. *From Untouchable to Dalit: Essays on the Ambedkar Movement*. New Delhi: Manohar, 1992. Print.

Chapter Two

Dalits and the Caste Question

In the previous chapter we discussed how 'Dalit' as a category is a product of the caste system in India. Although there have been a considerable number of studies on caste as an institution, with its corollary being untouchability, few efforts have succeeded in comprehending the phenomenon fully and clearly. Theories accounting for the genesis and persistence of the caste system are often exaggerated and hence misleading. Perhaps, the roots of the caste system are buried so deep that it has not been possible for scholars to arrive at a definite conclusion about its origin. Studies on the caste system and untouchability often remind one of the oft-quoted parable of six visually challenged men and the elephant, in which several hypotheses deal with only parts and neglect the whole. Keeping the difficulty of the task in mind, we will make an attempt to give an overview of the Indian caste system while focussing mainly on the issue of untouchability, which has a bearing on Dalit life-worlds.

It has always been difficult to define 'caste', perhaps due to its complex nature. Some scholars attempt to define caste in terms of class. But 'class' is basically an economic term generally applied to market-dominated societies where caste hardly plays any role. Others have compared 'caste' with non-class divisions such as 'race' and 'racism'. But 'caste' is certainly not 'race', though the very word 'caste' has its origin in a Portuguese word *casta* which means 'lineage' or 'race'. Still, the term 'caste' does evoke a picture of fixed statuses and occupations with social immobility firmly solidified by rules of endogamy. All these features are strictly backed by or based on religiously governed principles of 'purity' and 'pollution', which automatically render a social structure hierarchical. Thus, the caste system can be defined as an extreme form of social stratification. When did 'caste' as a social system come to be established in Indian society? Who invented this system as a social hierarchy? What were its repercussions for people and society at large? The following sections will try and address these questions so that we will be able to understand the relationship between caste and Dalit lives.

A BRIEF HISTORY OF CASTE

The Indus Civilisation

There are two opposing views concerning the origin of the caste system. One view is called the Western or historian's view, and the other, the brahminical view. The Western view is generally centred on the Aryan invasion theory and the consequent social oppression and enslavement of the native population. The brahminic view is a mythological–religious theory which sees caste as a result of divine sanctions, with its origin mainly in the Purusha sukta, a part of the Rig Veda. However, both views mostly rely on internal evidence found in the Vedas and the post-Vedic literature. A full account would require a look into the pre-Aryan period when, historians believe, there was no caste system in India.

The Indus Valley civilisation (of about 2500–1700 BCE) is believed to be the oldest civilisation that existed in India. Many historians are of the view that this civilisation belonged to the Dravidians. Though there are disputes about whether the Dravidians were aboriginal to India or had migrated from outside, it is believed that they had been living in India since at least about 4000 BCE – long before the Aryans came and settled down. Another point to support this theory is that the Indus Valley civilisation was urban in nature while Aryan culture was a relatively primitive non-urban culture. The Aryans were a nomadic, horse-riding, cattle-herding people who adopted many practices of the Dravidians and other indigenous groups that they came across.

The discovery of different types of houses in the Indus cities indicates the existence of simple class divisions among the people. In the main city, rulers, priests, businessmen and skilled workers used to live in houses while the poor used to live in huts outside the city. Tribals and 'menials' used to live still farther away from the city. The Indus Valley discoveries of blacksmithing techniques, mortar, food-grain stores and houses of workers are all evidence of the existence of a slave society. But there is nothing in these findings to enable one to construct a theory to prove that a caste system existed at that time. Referring to the Indus civilisation, Gail Omvedt, in her *Understanding Caste: From Buddha to Ambedkar and Beyond*, writes, 'With the script – if it is that – still undeciphered, little is known about the heart of this civilisation; it was widespread, impressive, relatively equalitarian, lacking weapons of war, and has left us only a few statuary relics, including a beautiful fragile dancing girl and an authoritative, bearded male, possibly a priest' (1).

The Role of the Aryans

Although debatable, the theory that the Aryans came and settled down in the region of the Punjab from their original home in Middle Asia, has gained a measure of acceptance. As mentioned earlier, they were nomadic, chariot-driving tribal groups who reared cattle. They were at a relatively primitive, non-urban stage of culture compared to the Indus Valley civilisation. However, they were essentially a race of warriors who were bold, hardy, superstitious adventurers who steadily extended their migrations, overcoming and sometimes mercilessly extirpating the aborigines who opposed their march, until they were able to establish powerful kingdoms in the Gangetic valley. Swami Dharma Theertha in *History of Hindu Imperialism* describes the ways and means by which the Aryans defeated the Dravidians, the inhabitants of the land. Theertha writes,

> Dominated by the military and predatory spirit, they (Aryans) lived the life of activity, adventure and enjoying of all the good things of the world. They invoked their gods . . . constantly to destroy the aboriginal tribes whom they contemptuously called "dark-skinned dasyus" and "rakshasas" (demons). Many hymns of the Rg Veda are fervent appeals to the gods to annihilate Dasyus. "We are surrounded on all sides by the Dasyus. They do not perform sacrifices. They are unbelievers. Their practices are all . . . different. They are mean! O! Destroyer of foes! Kill them, destroy the Dasa race" (Rg Veda, I,

> 100—8). . . . Health, wealth, prosperity and power in this world were the chief and almost sole concern of the Aryans, and to them religion was a means of acquiring these. (13)

Theertha's inferences are based mostly on the Vedas, which are considered to be the earliest documents that record the Aryan lives, culture and philosophy. Several historians have tried to read early Indian history with the help of the Vedas. One such historian is D. D. Kosambi who sees the Rig Veda as the source for the story of the Aryan invasion, destruction and conquest in India. In his book *The Culture and Civilization of Ancient India in Historical Outline* he substantiates the above view by saying that the decline of the Indus Valley civilisation, according to archaeological evidence, occurred around 1800 BCE and the actions described in the Rig Veda were practised around the same time. The rest of the Vedas were composed much later, probably about 900 BCE. It is during these Vedic times that a kind of social division – but not necessarily caste divisions as we know it today – was created, a structure which seems to be the forerunner of our social structure today.

In the Rig Veda, along with the distinction between *arya* and *dasa*, there is a division of society into three orders, brahmana, kshatriya and vaishya or *vis*. The first two broadly represented the two professions of poet-priest and warrior-chief. The third division was apparently a group comprising all the common people. Later, these three orders became the four divisions we know today – brahmin, kshatriya, vaishya and shudra. The introduction of the *chaturvarna* (four classes) is rendered in a metaphorical way in the creation myth of the Purusha sukta in the tenth mandala of the Rig Veda. It says that the creator produced the first community (the brahmins) from the mouth, the second (the kshatriyas) from the shoulders, the third (the vaishyas) from the thighs and the last (the shudras) from the feet.

Narayana, the famous rishi who sanctified Badrinath by his stay there, is supposed to be the author of the Purusha sukta – the first Indian attempt at a cosmogenic hypothesis. The sukta was most likely the first such text that theorised caste rules, which were later truly and deeply sown into the community with all the sanctity a religion could grant. This is borne out by the Aitreya Brahmana, which describes a brahmin as a 'receiver of gifts, a drinker of the soma, a seeker of food and liable to be removed at will', a vaishya as 'tributory to another to be believed on by another and to be repressed at will', and a shudra as 'a servant of another to be slain at will' (Murthy 7–8). The kshatriya is left out of this inventory of functions as he is the king and has command over all in his domain (Murthy 7–8).

It appears that the division of society under the four varnas was mainly job-oriented, with specific duties attached to each position. But, as is evident from their origin, it seems to be clear that the varnas were hierarchically placed for the first time during Vedic times. The Aryans were arranged into four varnas; the first three varnas called themselves *dwijas* (twice-born) and possibly the local gentry, who were friendly to the Aryans, were also included in this list (Mukherjee 37–63). Most of the occupational groups were probably included under the vaishya varna. The shudra varna, in all probability, comprised non-wealthy, conquered and hostile groups. This probably led to the conjecture that the *das/dasyu/rakshasa* of the Rig Veda formed the shudra varna.

Here a question arises: what made the Aryans suddenly divide people into four varnas, that too in a hierarchical order? In other words, what conditions made the caste system evolve on Indian soil? On this subject Harold Gould, an American sociologist, writes,

> Among the network of civilisations that ramified outward from the Middle East and populated the Euro-Asiatic river valleys after 5000 BC, India evolved a cultural system that carried it to its ultimate expression. By modelling ritual behaviour on the division of labour and ranking all occupational behaviour on a pollution scale, Hinduism provided the basis for the virtually unlimited permutation of Indian society into hereditary compartments ordained to perform their separate but interdependent religious and economic functions. The caste system was the result. (68)

While Gould ascribes the ascriptive conditions of the caste system to 'religious and economic functions', there are others, particularly Dalit writers, who advance different opinions. Jagjivan Ram suggests that it was purely political motives that led the Aryans to divide the people hierarchically because they wanted to 'maintain the purity of their blood'. Ram argues that the caste system was a by-product of political motivation which was then supported by religious sanctions. 'Colour-conscious Aryans, who regarded themselves as culturally superior, were anxious to maintain the purity of their blood. Under the impact of these forces the trivarnic society became chaturvarnic, and the latter spilt into a large number of castes and sub-castes within the framework of their fourfold system of society' (10).

The Aryan theory thus seems to involve several points: that Aryans came from outside and subjugated the indigenous people; that they destroyed the pre-existing Indus civilisation; and that the upper caste descended from Aryans and the lower castes, including shudras and Dalits, from the darker skinned non-Aryans. However, today practically no social scientist or historian accepts the Aryan theory as the only way to explain the origin of the caste system. Ambedkar too did not accept it, emphasising that caste was not a racial division but a division of different communities which the brahmins divided into 'high' and 'low' to keep power in their hands. However, it remains important because it is widely and popularly believed, and the majority of upper castes still see the Aryans as their ancestors.

The Consolidation of Caste Society and Untouchability

With the chaturvarnic order, Indian caste society gradually came to be established during the period 500 BCE to 500 CE. During this time many caste laws and restrictions were made so that the shudras would be kept deliberately away from the so-called *dwija* society and degrade them to the position of virtual slaves without rights of citizenship. These caste rules were mostly made by the brahmins with the active support of the orthodox kshatriya kings. Thus, the caste scheme proved to be a very effective instrument of domination and exploitation – for keeping the masses of people ignorant in order to make them submissive, and for keeping them weak by increasing divisions among them.

In the varna scheme of the Vedas there are only four orders and there is no mention of the untouchable groups. However, there are references in Vedic literature to groups such as the ayogavas, chandalas, nishadas and paulkasas who are outside the varna scheme and who seem to be despised. Over the centuries this hierarchy continued to be implemented so that at the bottom of the caste gradation such marginal groups became identified as 'asprushyas', the 'untouchables', with the lowest standing. Usually, they also had the lowest economic positions and were traditionally subjected to debilitating social and civil disabilities.

The practice of untouchability seems to have begun during Pushyamitra Sunga's rule (187 BCE onwards). Pushyamitra was a brahmin and the commander-in-chief of the last Mauryan king Bruhadatra, who was a shudra by caste. Pushyamitra is believed to have killed Bruhadatra and established a brahmin rule which continued till 800 CE. Fearing that the shudras would organise a revolt against his actions, Pushyamitra asked Manu, a brahmin pandit of his time, to do him a favour. In order to suppress the potential revolution, Manu codified a number of inhuman and unethical laws against the shudras in the name of religion. His work was later known as the Manushastra or *Manusmriti*. It is with the *Manusmriti* that the full elaboration of the caste hierarchy can be seen. This seems to have been the beginning of brahminism. During this time, brahmins were given the highest status in society and caste divisions were enforced by kings. The role of the king was seen to be protecting 'dharma' and dharma was now interpreted as *varnashrama dharma* or the law of the castes (*varna* meaning caste/group and *ashrama* meaning stages of life). To keep the interests of the upper caste intact, this *varnashrama dharma* was often supported, propagated and reinterpreted through the Upanishads, the sutras, the smritis, and the puranas, which are collectively known as the Dharma shastra today.

Thus, through the following centuries, the Dharma shastra imposed a series of social, political, economic and religious restrictions on the lower castes, making the 'untouchables' completely dependent on those above them. As a result, the 'untouchables' lived a life of physical degradation and personal and social humiliation. They were relegated to 'menial' occupations.

They lived outside the village and fed on the leftovers of high-caste people. Physical contact with 'untouchables' was said to be 'polluting' and even their shadows were considered defiling. Even as late as the early part of the twentieth century, 'untouchables' had no access to public facilities such as wells, rivers, roads, schools, and markets. Perverted practices such as forcing 'untouchables' to wear a pot round their necks to catch their saliva, or to tie a broom behind them to sweep away their footprints, reinforced the idea of the 'untouchables' as 'polluting' and 'polluted'. All these forced conditions made the 'untouchables' deprived and one of the most depressed sections of human beings in India. As a result of such practices they remained socially backward, economically impoverished and politically at the mercy of the upper castes. How long did such practices continue? Was there no protest against the caste system?

PROTESTS AGAINST CASTE

Lokayata

Eventually, protests against caste practices came from various quarters. At different point of times in history, the institution of caste was questioned by philosophers and reformers whose ideas would create the background for either new religions or new systems of thought that challenged caste. The first challenge to the caste system came from a group of rationalists known as Lokayata, which literally means 'restricted to the world of common experience or Charvakas' (Chattopadhyaya 1) which came to be established in sixth century BCE. Headed by the famous materialist philosopher Charvaka, the movement revolted against the slave system, caste exploitation and the existence of God. The Lokayata propagated a materialistic philosophy as opposed to the idealism of the Upanishads and the Vedas. They preached the abolition of slavery, and espoused rational behaviour and beliefs that rejected all forms of sacrifices, rituals and ceremonies. Thus, the Lokayata emerged as a progressive and optimistic philosophy supporting the cause of oppressed people.

Jainism and Buddhism

During the sixth century BCE, both Jainism and Buddhism set about questioning brahminic orthodoxy. Religious scriptures were scrutinised to interrogate the truth. Although, compared to Buddhism, Jainism did not do much for the oppressed class of people – for the simple reason that it spread mainly among traders and businessmen – nevertheless it made a dent in brahminism (Theertha 94).

In a sense, Gautama Buddha was the first social revolutionary who challenged Vedantic philosophy and rejected the authority of the Vedas. His simple way of preaching righteousness of conduct over social tyranny, slavery and inequality, made his philosophy appealing to the common people. The Buddha did not prevent people of any caste or class from becoming his followers. 'Untouchables' could find a respectable place in society for the first time by embracing Buddhism. The Buddha invited the poorest and the lowliest to live and learn with princes and merchants, billionaires and brahmins in the brotherhood of his order. A humble craftsman or barber could rise to be a philosopher and teacher in the noble scheme of the Buddha.

It is unfortunate that in spite of its radical philosophy, Buddhism lost its battle with brahminism, which ended up appropriating it. As a result, the Buddha was given a high place in the Hindu pantheon as an *avatara* of Vishnu. This happened because the brahmins perceived the popularity of Buddhism as a threat to their entrenched position and made efforts to suborn it.

Once Buddhism started declining, Hinduism laid a renewed emphasis on caste distinctions. And it was brahminism, the militant part of Hinduism (Chatterjee 2010), which took charge of the efforts to reinforce these divisions. It is believed that Hindu reformers such as Kumarilabhatt (around 750 CE), Adi Sankaracharya (born in 788 CE), Ramanujacharya (twelfth century CE) and Madhavacharya (thirteenth century CE) played a great role in attacking the various tenets of Buddhism and at the same time, propagating and consolidating the practices of Hinduism.

Bhakti Movement

In the medieval period, the Bhakti movement (roughly from the eighth to eighteenth century CE), which threw up radical thinkers and mystic reformers, was yet another force that challenged the varna system and stratification of human society on the basis of caste. The movement cut across barriers of caste, creed, language and religion. Many of the well-known poets, singers and saints in the Bhakti cults were from lower castes. Namdev (1270–1350 CE) belonged to the shimphi (tailor) caste from Maharashtra; Chokhamela (thirteenth–fourteenth century CE) was a mahar (untouchable), also from Maharashtra; Kabir (fifteenth century CE) was a weaver from Uttar Pradesh; Raidas (a contemporary of Kabir's) was a cobbler from Uttar Pradesh; Sena (another contemporary of Kabir's) was a barber from the same region; Tukaram (born in 1608 CE) was a kunbi (peasant) from Maharashtra. The languages these saint–poets used for their songs, *dohas* and *abhangs* were the local languages spoken by the common people and very often they used metaphors connected with their daily work. Though there is no evidence to suggest that Chokhamela ever protested against the traditional limits of mahar village work, the internal evidence in his *abhangs* suggests some protest against the concept of untouchability. Kabir's strong note of dissent and protest against the existing reality, the glaring disparity between the rich and poor, the discrimination by brahmins and high-caste Hindus towards the lower castes, especially the 'untouchables', and his emphasis on a direct relationship with God without the mediation of brahmins and the mullahs, that is, the clerics whom he ridicules as greedy and ignorant, had a profound impact on society. Surdas (1483–1563 CE) graphically described the hard life of the peasants and the oppressions of the local officials, landholders and even high officials such as the *wazir*. There were other saint–poets who took up caste, class and gender issues in their own way and initiated public discussions around such issues.

Of late, the Bhakti movement has been critically examined in terms of its various contributions to caste hierarchies in India. While many historians and literary critics have seen Bhakti literature as an incipient movement for social protest due to this low-caste base and often bitter descriptions of social oppression, others deny such an interpretation. There are various and ambivalent readings of this movement. Finally, what emerges from the different studies is the diversity and heterogeneity of the Bhakti movement. It spread across several centuries and a vast geographical area; it was also expressed in many languages and had a significant impact on the way caste and religion as institutions were viewed.

The Caste System and Islam

One must note that even during the Muslim rule in India (800–1600 CE), brahminism made its presence felt. The Muslim rulers played the same role as the Hindu kings in enforcing the rules of *varnashrama dharma* (Jiloha 81). Aware of the minority status of their religion, Muslim rulers adopted the policy of not interfering with Hindu society and allowed the brahmins to interpret religion in their own way. This provided them with an opportunity to enforce caste laws and restrictions in different walks of life. Jiloha writes,

> Forcible conversion of caste-Hindus to Islam also took place which helped Hinduism to become more orthodox, more strict in caste rules such as purdah system and its mobility toward Islam created many a non-caste professions which were adopted by neo-Muslims with a fair degree of acceptance in Islam. The fear of defilement closed those occupations to the Hindus; this fear spread and became general among the inferior population owing to the religious influence of the immigrants and of their priests. The sections were graded according to the degree of impurity. (78–79)

The conditions of the untouchables and other lower-caste people in the Hindu community remained the same as before during the Muslim period. Probably as a protest against this continuing discrimination, a sizeable number of Hindus, mostly from the 'untouchables' and backward castes, converted to Islam. The moplahs of Malabar and communities from Chittagong in Bangladesh are examples of en masse conversions to Islam. Only some of the so-called lower ranks, mainly artisans and wage earners (the real producers of wealth), willingly embraced Islam, attracted by its democratic structure and fraternal approach. Jiloha says,

> As minorities cannot resist absorbing the characteristics of majority, Muslims were influenced by Hindus and as a consequence Muslims too started looking down upon untouchables the way caste-Hindus were doing. To avoid it there was a large-scale conversion of untouchables to Islam which provided a very fertile ground for the spread of Islam as well as an alternative to untouchables, to lead a better life, to participate in some way to the advantage of religious identification. (78)

Compared to Hinduism, Islam granted relative equality to everyone irrespective of caste or class status. Islam seemed to provide every follower of the Prophet opportunities to rise to any position according to one's own ability. Mattison Mines finds at least four social divisions among Tamil Muslims: labbai, rawther, marakayar, and kayalar. He writes about them thus; 'All four sub-divisions are of approximately equal status. Status socio-grams, movable card ranking and observations of interaction among members of different subdivisions reveal that, unlike Hindu castes, the Muslim subdivisions are not ranked . . . but ranking exists on the level of the individual and is based primarily on the individual's conduct, his age, wealth, personal character and religiousness' (159–70). In 1981, the conversion of more than two hundred Dalit families in Meenakshipuram, Tamil Nadu, indicated a renewal of faith in Islam among marginal people.

CASTE DURING BRITISH RULE

By the end of the eighteenth century, the Bhakti movement was dying out and Indian society had become rigid and stratified. It is at this juncture that India came directly in contact with the British. As rulers the British studied the nature of Indian society and different ways of life of its people. Through exploration, excavation, formulation and tabulation, they tried to understand the past and present of India, its landscape and history. This knowledge was an important element in understanding and controlling the country. The impact of British rule in India as seen by Marc Galanter was:

> Conditions of peace, new communications, new economic activities, new kinds of employment, a new legal system,

> a new system of property relations, and new ideas brought in their train new opportunities and new modes of mobility. Old powers and prerogatives were abolished; occupations and learning were rendered obsolete or marginal; new opportunities for gain and advancement were introduced; power and access to it were redistributed (but), the utilisation of these new opportunities was biased by the existing distribution of resources and by the network of kinship and community which offered access to them. (18)

Galanter's observations would suggest that, in spite of the 'newness' in administration, infrastructure, economy, etc., British rule tended to reproduce the old hierarchies in many spheres, including the army. Thus, the upper castes continued to enjoy power in spite of the fact that India was administered by the British.

During British rule, and particularly in the nineteenth century, Christian missionaries were important agents of change in the lives of the untouchables. The missionaries were pragmatists. They gave the untouchables only such things which would immediately grant them social status and self-esteem. They built as many churches as they built schools and hospitals, in inaccessible and remote tribal areas. Bihar, Madhya Pradesh, West Bengal and the whole of the Northeast came noticeably under the influence of the missionaries. As in Africa, the coastal regions in India also became centres of missionary activity. As a result, coastal states such as Kerala and the coastal parts of Karnataka and Tamil Nadu saw immediate social, educational and economic changes. Duncan B. Forrester, one of the experts on conversion, writes,

> New educational opportunities gradually (be)came available to converts, and changes in life-style became accepted. Converts were accepted to give up the eating carrion and drinking alcohol, were encouraged to show their greater cleanliness, and soon found it possible to enter a variety of occupations which had hitherto been closed to them, such as school teaching, or work in one of the mission industries. (78)

These missionary interventions in India brought several changes in the lives of their Dalit converts. Among other things, access to education gave them a sense of understanding about their lives and their social context, which later helped them to begin to articulate their voice.

Today, missionary activities have come to a standstill due to various reasons (Joshi). The withdrawal of government support which they enjoyed during colonial rule and the predominance of religion and caste in national and local politics seem to have curtailed missionary activities in India. Evidence from the tribal belts of Bihar, Jharkhand, Odisha, Chhattisgarh and Madhya Pradesh seem to suggest that many churches have come under severe threat and attacks from Hindu fundamentalist groups. Many Christians were reconverted to Hinduism under threat and by compulsion. Newspapers have reported that Hindu fundamentalist groups have launched movements to reconvert the Dalits and Adivasis who have changed their faiths by embracing other religions. These neo-converts though have nothing to cheer about because after their re-conversion they are still looked down upon by upper-caste Hindus. Also, though conversion to Christianity, Islam or other religions has uplifted Dalits, caste markers and prejudices continue to be reinforced even in their new communities. These converts are still known as Dalit Christians, Dalit Muslims, etc. More importantly, sub-caste distinctions (in names, occupation and physical addresses) continue to be upheld.

Of course, conversion had become a political issue long before the recent Hindutva wave tightened its hold on the polity. Improvement of social and economic conditions of the large number of outcastes through conversion to non-Hindu religions was seen as a threat to the power of the dominant Hindu society. For instance, the major Hindu reform movements of the earlier century, such as Brahmo Samaj, Prarthana Samaj and Arya Samaj, paid serious attention to the problem of caste and conversion. Let us briefly look at these social movements.

SOCIAL REFORM MOVEMENTS

All through the nineteenth century the building of roads and railways, introduction of postal services and telegraph, the advent of the printing press, and the setting up of many industries by the

British helped India organise itself in new ways through improved communications. Besides, the influence of Enlightenment brought new secular and democratic ideas, which led to a number of reform movements in India, especially with regard to Hinduism. The first important reform movement in Hinduism, the Brahmo Samaj, was initiated by Raja Rammohan Roy (1792–1833) in 1828. Under its influence, what were seen as meaningless rituals of pantheistic worship were given up. Roy rejected the doctrines of *karma* and *samskara*, and thereby challenged the basic dogma of Hinduism. At the same time he acted as a reformer of Hindu religion by preaching and practising the brotherhood of man. Though it attacked some of the evils of the caste system, the Brahmo Samaj seems to have concentrated more on issues pertaining to the upper castes, for example, *sati*, child marriage, widow remarriage, etc. Those who felt attracted towards this new version of Hinduism were mainly the educated and westernised class, and the movement remained confined largely to Bengal.

Later in the century, in the northern part of the country, the Arya Samaj, founded by Dayanand Saraswati (1834–83) in 1857, called for Hindus to 'Go back to the Veda' (Mani 213). It meant delving into the past to facilitate a religious revival in order to gain self-respect. The Arya Samaj attempted to restore the glories of Hinduism and to counter the influence of Christianity and Western values. To achieve this goal Dayanand Saraswati wished to reform the caste system and abandon the puranas and shastras. He also opposed caste restrictions, child marriage, the purdah system, conversion and illiteracy. He advocated the abolition of untouchability, emancipation of women, and the development of education in Sanskrit and Hindi. He also preached worship of a single god and condemned polytheism.

Dayanand Saraswati believed that the spread of foreign ideology and the spread of other faiths, particularly that of Islam and Christianity, were dangerous for India. He preached against both these religions and introduced proselytisation into Hinduism for the first time. As a result, even a non-Hindu could convert to Hinduism. He also organised a *shuddhi* movement where persecuted untouchables were given sacred threads to wear like the three upper castes, to become 'caste Hindus'. However, the agenda of the Arya

Samaj, like that of the Brahmo Samaj, was limited to reforming Hinduism and hence it did not widely spread across all castes.

Ramakrishna Paramhansa (1834–86), though not a social reformer (he was a mystic), abhorred the practice of untouchability. He said that no one was born high or low and declared that though born in a brahmin family, he would, in truth, be at home with a scavenger. During the early stages of his penance, he found he could not overcome the pride and arrogance of his superior birth (Ghose 212). In order to reform this disturbing trait in himself, it is said, he went one day to the hovel of an untouchable and swept the courtyard, not with a broom but with his own long hair.

Ramakrishna's disciple, Swami Vivekananda (1862–1902) did not mince words while condemning untouchability in unequivocal terms. According to him, untouchability was a strange and astounding belief and did not form part of Hindu religion. It was neither in the Vedas nor in the puranas and yet had become the ruling 'dharma' to the entire exclusion of all the great principles taught by Hinduism. He was of the view that untouchability was the cause of India's downfall and made Indians cowardly and thoroughly contemptible (Brodov). Vivekananda prescribes an ideal Indian society where the best qualities of all the four castes – brahmin (knowledge), kshatriya (valour), vaishya (business acumen) and shudra (physical work) – are integrated and their flaws are removed. This view of Vivekananda seems to be the same as that of the other religious reformers mentioned earlier.

During the freedom struggle, leaders like Bal Gangadhar Tilak too castigated untouchability. Tilak, for example, believed that untouchability had no connection with Vedic dharma and it was the machinations of ancient brahmins that gave birth to untouchability. He further observed that untouchability was a sin against God and he could not respect a God who favoured religious sanctions against a section of people by calling them 'untouchables' (Mani 236).

Tilak was a chitpavan brahmin by caste and wrote a book called *Gita rahasya*, supporting Hinduism but criticising 'brahmanism'. It is said that his book, especially dealing with the origin of the Aryans, was so appreciated by Queen Victoria that she freed him from prison (which he had been sentenced to because of his political activities). Later, Tilak introduced the Ganapati as well as Shivaji festivals as annual celebrations, to unify the Hindus in his home state of Maharashtra. The attempt was a great success. Though the tradition of celebrating these festivals is still continued in and around Maharashtra, these practices are now being manipulated by Hindu fundamentalists to play caste politics.

The Role of M. K. Gandhi

In the twentieth century, the emergence of Gandhi into the Indian political scene brought about a perceptible change in Hindu society. M. K. Gandhi (1867–1948) believed that untouchability was an excrescence, a pathological growth that had nothing to do with the essential nature of the caste system which was a framework for the division of labour. Defending the Indian caste system, Gandhi writes,

> The spirit behind caste is not one of arrogant superiority; it is the classification of different systems of self-culture. It is the best possible adjustment of social stability and progress. Just as the spirit of the family is inclusive of those who love each other and are wedded to each other by ties of blood and relation, caste also tries to include families of a particular way of purity of life (not standard of life, meaning by this term, economic standard of life). . . . Caste does not connote superiority or inferiority. It simply recognizes different outlooks and corresponding modes of life. . . . (174–75)

Gandhi maintained that caste had existed in the past without untouchability and that the notion of untouchability could be purged from it without damages to its fundamental design. Gandhi advocated a purified *varnashrama dharma* in which 'untouchables' would be restored to their rightful place as shudras (Gandhi). Gandhi's idea of *varnashrama dharma* has invited much criticism. The idea that children should follow their fathers' professions seems to be alright for the three upper castes, that is, brahmins, kshatriyas and vaishyas, but not for shudras and ati-shudras. Since the traditional duties of shudras and ati-shudras are mainly composed of menial and physically dirty work (such as scavenging), Gandhi's belief in the *chaturvarna* system seems to be quite problematic. Instead of being liberated from the rigidities of caste occupation, under this reconceptualisation they are being further enslaved to the system. This seems to contradict the democratic idea that the people at the receiving end of injustice and oppression must get social justice irrespective of their caste, class or religion.

Thus, the reform movements in India which began with Raja Rammohan Roy and continued till Gandhi were mostly led by the upper-caste men who were worried about the 'decadent' Hinduism of their day. Though all of them talked about social equality among other things, their main objectives were to modify Hinduism in keeping with an idealised Vedic period. This led to a period called the Indian 'Renaissance' or 'reawakening'.

NON-BRAHMIN MOVEMENTS

While upper-caste reformism wanted to modify and update Hinduism, there was another movement going on at the same time that was organised mostly by lower-caste leaders. It is known as the 'Non-brahmin Movement', or 'the Enlightenment'. The leaders of the Enlightenment talked about creating a new society with a new religion that was based on the universal ideas of 'liberty, equality and fraternity' as put forward by the thinkers of the French Revolution in 1789. Jotibarao Phule, E. V. Ramasamy Naicker (better known as Periyar), Narayana Guru and B. R. Ambedkar are the prominent figures of this movement.

Jotibarao Phule

The origin of the Non-brahmin Movement, otherwise known as the 'anti-caste movement', started with Jotibarao Phule in Maharashtra. Phule, a shudra who hailed from the mali (gardener) community, attacked the caste system and the continuing dominion of the brahmins over the lower castes. He attempted to demystify several Hindu concepts. The Hindu god Brahma, for him, was not a creator of the world but a stereotypical brahmin – an avaricious, cunning and secretive Aryan chieftain who not only waged wars against the natives but also wrote Vedic texts to protect the vested interests of the invaders. Phule writes of Brahma thus:

> . . . Brahma succeeded Waman as their Chieftain. He was very obdurate. He conquered our ancestors here and enslaved them (turned them into his vassals). He promulgated many iniquitous regulations so as to create a permanent rift between the Aryans and the conquered natives. After Brahma's death, the Aryans came to be known as "Brahmins", superseding their old name – Aryans. Officers like Manu who succeeded Brahma later on were anxious to maintain the sanctity of the regulations laid down by Brahma. Hence they composed many imaginary stories about Brahma. (4)

Phule felt that the only way the awareness of caste and an anti-caste consciousness could be inculcated in the oppressed was through education. In order for that to happen, it was necessary to fight against the upper-caste monopoly on education systems and institutions. To start off his movement, in 1848 Phule opened a school for the girl children of 'untouchables', the first of its kind, striking at the root of caste hegemony. In 1853, he established the 'society for the teaching of knowledge' to mahars, mangs, and other lower castes (Keer). In 1873, Phule established the Satyashodhak Samaj (Society for Truth Seekers), an organisation which proclaimed the need to save the lower castes from the 'hypocritical Brahmans and their opportunistic scriptures' (O'Hanlon 230).

Phule criticised the brahmin community for their evil practices of child marriage and shaving the heads of widows. He encouraged widow remarriage. He also tried to understand and explain the origin of the caste system. According to him, 'the prohibition, in the writing of Manu, of the education of the Shudras arose out of the fear lest the Shudras should remember their former greatness, and then rebel against their authority' (Phule 37).

Phule's movement was largely based in rural areas. It attacked the caste system, called for the usage of Marathi vernacular rather than English in schools, and claimed to speak for the 'Bahujan Samaj' (majority) against the 'Sethji-Bhatjis' (moneylenders and brahmins). Phule rejected the tenets of Hinduism and other religions based on holy books, prophets and so-called divine utterances, and advocated an ethics-based monotheistic religion.

Narayana Guru

Narayana Guru is yet another contributor to the Non-brahmin Movement, who championed the cause of all the downtrodden, including 'untouchables'. He was the founder of the Sri Narayana Dharma Paripalana Yogam (SNDP) movement, which originated among the ezhavas (toddy tappers) of Kerala in the late nineteenth century. The ezhavas were considered 'untouchables' in the traditional caste hierarchy in Kerala. As a result, they suffered from many restrictions and were not allowed to worship in the temples of caste Hindus. Toddy-tapping was considered to be a polluting occupation. The ezhava women could not cover their breasts and no one from this community could either wear footwear or build *pukka* houses till the 1940s.

Narayana Guru did not like the idea of people having different castes, religions and gods. In order to realise this philosophy, he undertook some concrete social actions. Guru's slogan was, 'For man there is only one religion; only one caste; and only one God' (Kumar 140), because he was against several religions, castes and gods which divided people. Initially he set up a Shiva temple for untouchables. But later on he built many temples dedicated to several gods and goddesses so that untouchables could worship them, and trained an order of monks, priests and household disciples (that is, disciples who could marry and have children and yet be a part of the temple structure). The temples he and his followers built were open to the lower castes. He preached that worship of God should not be denied to any individual or caste group: the denial of worship or access to god was an offence against god (Kunhappa). Narayana Guru also appointed 'untouchables' as cooks or bearers and tried to give them equal opportunities in all the organisations he set up. As part of his reformatory process he asked his followers to abstain from eating meat and drinking liquor, because he felt that the idea of purity was needed to have access to God. He must have been influenced by the Hindu idea of prohibition. He also evolved simpler wedding rites that did away with expensive and meaningless rituals. All these were meant to register an ideological protest against brahminical hierarchy and their notions of pollution. Narayana

Guru was responsible for a thorough transformation of the style of life of the ezhavas, and created a paradigm shift in religious beliefs, rituals and outlook.

E. V. Ramasamy Naicker

The Non-brahmin Movement in Tamil Nadu came vigorously alive with the aggressive leadership of E. V. Ramasamy Naicker (1879–1973), popularly known as Periyar. Periyar began his Self-Respect Movement in 1925 and its primary objective was to discard the priestly service of the brahmins and their value-systems by resisting the tenets of Hinduism. While seeking a basic change in the traditional social system, Periyar wanted to establish an entirely new pattern of values in which all people, irrespective of their caste, creed or sex, could enjoy equal self-respect. Citing the racial dispute theory – that the migrant Aryans conquered the subjugated indigenous Dravidians – Periyar emphasised that Dravidian culture was far superior to the brahminical Aryan culture. He used this argument to mobilise mass support, with 'untouchables', women, rural youth and the uneducated masses.

As a part of his Non-brahmin Movement, Periyar advocated the need for a separate non-brahmin or Dravidian country. In 1944, the Dravida Kazhagam came into being with its primary demand being a separate non-brahmin Dravidian nation. It later went on to become a political party. The Self-Respect Movement later broke down into many separate entities because of internal politicking.

B. R. Ambedkar

It was B. R. Ambedkar, the architect of Indian Constitution, who made significant contributions to the anti-caste movement at a national level. An 'untouchable' himself, Ambedkar championed the cause of the 'broken men', as he termed Indian 'untouchables', and fought relentlessly throughout his life to ensure equality, social justice, self-respect and freedom for them. Ambedkar stood for the social liberation, economic emancipation and political advancement of the downtrodden, a task that had never been undertaken by any high-caste Hindu leader with so much vigour and force. That is why perhaps, M. K. Gandhi described him as 'fierce and fearless' and Jawaharlal Nehru acclaimed him as a 'symbol of revolt against all the oppressing features of Hindu society'.

A radical reconstruction of Indian society, as Ambedkar imagined it, could not happen without the intensification of the caste/class struggle. Since Hinduism is founded on scriptures which sanctioned the caste-based social order, a just solution could only be possible through the annihilation of the Indian caste system. Ambedkar launched several protest movements to achieve this. As early as 1927, he started a Marathi fortnightly, *Bahishkrit Bharat,* to give a voice to millions of voiceless people. In the same year he also established the Samaj Samata Sangh (Association for Social Equality) to achieve social equality among untouchables and to encourage inter-caste marriage, among other objectives. In 1930, the temple entry movement was launched with an attempt to enter the Kala Ram Mandir at Nasik. The *Janata*, a weekly, was started by Ambedkar during this period. He formed the Samata Sainik Dal (Social Equality Army) to remove values which fostered an anti-human attitude in the name of traditional or cultural heritage. Apart from these, Ambedkar also established several educational institutes and political parties and also published periodicals and journals as part of his movement.

The sole motive of Ambedkar's movement was to establish the equal status of all classes and castes in religious, social, economic and political spheres, thus offering 'untouchables' an opportunity to rise up the ladder of life and creating conducive conditions for their advancement. Ambedkar came to realise that for the complete uplifting of the downtrodden to happen, securing political power was a necessity. Otherwise it would not be possible for this suppressed section of Indian society to completely wipe out all the social, legal and cultural disabilities from which they suffered. That is why his slogan was, 'Be a ruling race'. Unfortunately, the political power which Ambedkar wanted for the 'untouchables' during British rule could not be obtained due to the stiff resistance of the Congress with its caste-Hindu character. Ambedkar characterised the Congress as a 'full-blooded and blue-blooded Hindu body' (Ambedkar 186). Like most other Dalit and many non-brahmin leaders of his day, he believed that the Congress leadership was in the hands of upper-caste conservatives who actively opposed Dalit demands. Thus, Dalits, along with Muslims, asked for special representation and separate electorates to avoid being overshadowed by caste-Hindu nationalists and their agenda.

As the architect of the Indian Constitution, Ambedkar worked hard for a new constitutional order based on equality and social justice. However, his dream is yet to materialise more than six decades after the establishment of the Constitution. The continuing discrimination and atrocities perpetrated by other castes on Dalits stands testament to the non-actualisation of his dream.

Dismayed and frustrated with the negative attitude of upper-caste Hindus, Ambedkar, towards the end of his life, rejected Hinduism and embraced Buddhism, which advocated a casteless and classless society. The Buddha's opposition to human exploitation is perhaps the main reason for why Ambedkar found Buddhism to be a viable alternative to Hinduism.

Apart from Phule, Narayana Guru, Periyar and Ambedkar there were other non-brahmin leaders who led Non-brahmin movements in their respective states. Harichand Biswas (1812–77) in Bengal, Bhima Bhoi (around 1855–94) in Odisha, Iyothee Thass (1845–1914) in Tamil Nadu, Swami Achhutanad Parihar (1869–1933) in Uttar Pradesh, Mangu Ram Mugowalia (1886–1980) in Punjab and Ayyankali (1863–1941) in Kerala were some of the more prominent individuals who waged war against caste oppression. Many of them were creative writers who, through their writings, influenced the reading public. Thus, with their articulation of Dalit subjectivity, 'Dalit discourse' became a part of the larger public sphere.

DALITS IN POST-INDEPENDENCE INDIA

Despite the legal abolition of untouchability in independent India (the Untouchability Offences Act was passed in 1955, followed by the Protection of Civil Rights [PCR] Act in 1976), the effects of caste discrimination prevail to this day. The upper castes possess most of the social, economic and political power while the lower castes continue to be subordinated. The 'untouchables' who constitute the lowest strata are naturally in the most disadvantaged situation. Kancha Ilaiah, reviewing the post-Independence caste phenomenon, writes,

> By 1947 itself an all India "upper caste elite" – the new bhadralok – was to take over the whole range of post-colonial political institutions. From the village institutions of patel and patwari to tehsil offices, collectorates, State and Central Secretariats; from gram panchayats to municipalities, zilla parishads to state legislatures and the central Parliament, each institution was made the preserve of the "upper" caste forces, with Brahmins being in the lead in many of these institutions. The neo-Kshatriyas, while co-existing with them, accepted their hegemonic role in law-making and interpreting history. (49)

After the British left India, the upper castes took over and occupied all positions of consequence in the public sphere and cemented their dominion over the lower castes and Dalits. As a result, Dalits in rural India are still struggling to assert themselves amidst the orthodox rural caste structure, while their urban counterparts are a little better off being educated, mobilised and organised, and are uniting to agitate against the various caste discriminations practised against them. But such attempts made by Dalits have been easily suppressed and various kinds of atrocities have been inflicted upon them to curb their power. What is even more shocking is that, in recent times, Dalits have become the victims of state-sponsored violence which is carried out subtly but systematically in the guise of various developmental programmes. To quote Ilaiah,

> In post-colonial India, in the name of Congress democratic rule, the Hindus came to power both at Delhi and at the provincial headquarters. Parliamentary democracy in essence became brahminical democracy. Within no time the colonial bureaucracy was transformed into a brahminical bureaucracy. The same brahminical forces transformed themselves to suit an emerging global capitalism. They recast their Sanskritized life-style to anglicized life-styles, reshaping themselves, to live a semi-capitalist (and at the same time brahminical) life. Their anglicization did not undermine their casteized (casteist) authoritarianism. All apex power centres in the country were brahminized and the power of the bureaucracy greatly

> extended. Because of their anglicization quite a few of them were integrated into the global techno-economic market. Such top brahminical elites were basically unconcerned with the development of the rural economy because it would result in changing the conditions of the Dalit-bahujan masses and thus new social forces might emerge. Thus the anglicized brahminical class also became an anti-development social force. (51–52)

However, these anti-development forces have now become the subject of scrutiny. Since a considerable number of Dalits are now educated, debates on caste issues are heard in the public sphere more often than earlier. This is because Dalit subjectivity now has come to such a stage that upper-caste intellectuals can no longer ignore it. Only when we listen to Dalit expressions of self can we gauge the way Dalit creativity is writing a new history.

CONCLUSION

In ancient times, powerful communities such as the brahmins and kshatriyas invented 'caste' to exploit and oppress the so-called lower castes by manipulating power. This caste hegemony continues to this day. If we look at Indian history, protests against caste were staged almost all through recorded times – the Charvakas and the Buddha in the ancient era, Bhakti saint–poets like Kabir, Nanak, Chokhamela and Ravidas in medieval times, and non-brahmin leaders like Jotibarao Phule, Narayana Guru, Periyar and B. R. Ambedkar in modern times. While these non-brahmin leaders demanded equality and dignity from caste society, their counterparts, the upper-caste reformers, worked primarily for their own constituencies. It was in 1972 that the Dalit Panthers Movement kick-started the modern, well-organised Dalit movement demanding freedom from caste oppressions. It is no surprise that this new social movement began in Maharashtra, the homeland of Ambedkar who fought for the rights, liberties and equalities of the downtrodden throughout his life. The emergence of a Dalit consciousness was the main reason for the rise of the Dalit movement and Dalit literature. The emergence of Dalit literature can be seen as a corollary to this dynamic Dalit movement. But what are the other factors that led to the coming of Dalit literature? Who played the role of the initiator? What are its special features? How was it received? We will try to look for answers to these questions in our next chapter.

REFERENCES

Ambedkar B. R. *What Congress and Gandhi have Done for Untouchables*. Bombay: Thacker and Co, 1945. Print.

Brodov, V. *Indian Philosophy in Modern Times*. Moscow: Progress Publishers, 1984. Print.

Chatterjee, Angana. *Violent Gods: Hindu Nationalism in India's Present, Narratives from Orissa*. Gurgaon: Three Essays Collective, 2010. Print.

Chattopadhyaya, D. P. *Lokayata: A Study of Ancient Indian Materialism*. Delhi: People's Publishing House, 1992. Print.

Forrester, Duncan B. *Caste and Christianity: Attitudes and Policies on Caste of Anglo-Saxon Protestant Missions in India*. London: Clarion Press, 1980. Print

Galanter, Marc. *Competing Equalities: Law and the Backward Classes in India*. Delhi: Oxford UP, 1994. Print.

Gandhi, M. K. *Collected Works of Mahatma Gandhi*. Vol. XIX. Delhi: The Publications Division, Ministry of Information and Broadcasting, Government of India, 1966. Print.

Ghose, Shankar. *The Western Impact in Indian Politics*. New Delhi: Allied Publishers, 1967. Print.

Gould, Harold A. *The Hindu Caste System*. Delhi: Chanakya Publications, 1987. Print.

Ilaiah, Kancha. *Why I am Not a Hindu: A Sudra Critique of Hindutva Philosophy, Culture and Political Economy?* Calcutta: Samya, 1996. Print.

Jiloha, R. C. *The Native Indian: In Search of Identity*. New Delhi: Blumoon Books, 1995. Print.

Joshi, Shashi. *Mission, Religion and Caste: Themes in the History of Christianity in India*, Shimla. Indian Institute of Advanced Study, 2010. Print.

Keer, Dhananjay. *Mahatma Jotirao Phule: Father of Our Social Revolution*. Bombay: Popular Prakashan, 2000. Print.

Kosambi, D. D. *The Culture and Civilisation of Ancient India in Historical Outline*. Delhi: Vikas, 1965. Print.

Kumar, Raj. *Dalit Personal Narratives.* Delhi: Orient BlackSwan, 2010. Print.

Kunhappa, Murkot. *Sree Narayana Guru*. Delhi: National Book Trust, 1988. Print.

Mani, Braj Ranjan. *Debrahmanising History: Dominance and Resistance in Indian Society*. New Delhi: Manohar, 2005. Print.

Mines, Mattison. 'Social Stratification among Muslim Tamils in Tamil Nadu, South India'. *Caste and Social Stratification among Muslims in India*. Ed. Imtiaz Ahmad. New Delhi: Manohar, 1978. Print. 159–170.

Mukherjee, Prabhati. *Beyond the Four Varnas: The Untouchables in India*. Shimla: Indian Institute of Advanced Study, 1988. Print.

Murthy, B. S. *Depressed and Oppressed*. New Delhi: S. Chand and Co., 1971. Print.

O' Hanlon, Rosalind. *Caste, Conflict and Ideology: Mahatma Jotirao Phule and Low Caste Protest in Nineteenth-Century Western India*. Cambridge: Cambridge UP, 1985. Print.

Omvedt, Gail. *Understanding Caste: From Buddha to Ambedkar and Beyond* New Delhi: Orient BlackSwan, 2011. Print.

Phule, Jotirao. *Collected Works of Mahatma Jotirao Phule.* Trans. P. G. Patil. 2 vols. Bombay: Education Department, Government of Maharashtra, 1991. Print.

Ram, Jagjivan. *Caste Challenge in India*. New Delhi: Vision Books, 1980. Print.

Theertha, Swami Dharma. *History of Hindu Imperialism*. 1941. Madras: Dalit Educational Literature Centre, 1992. Print.

Chapter Three

The Emergence of Dalit Literature

Although Indian society has, for centuries, been among the most hierarchical civilisations in the world (with a clear gradation in the exercise of power and privilege), the literatures of this country, until very recently, have never focused on the problem of inequality born out of the caste system. One of the reasons has been that the pen (both metaphorical and literal) has, by and large, been in the hands of those who have wielded power. Those outside the grid of authority and agency have generally been rendered invisible in the canonised literary texts of India. It is only towards the end of the nineteenth century that a few unusual novels take up the theme of social oppression as their major concern. Now, in the twentieth and twenty-first centuries, there is gradually a growing awareness in literature of those who have so far remained outside the threshold of mainstream Indian society: the outcastes, the landless, the dispossessed and the indigenous. This chapter will specifically look at the process through which 'Dalit literature' emerged. When did it take shape? What was the historical moment that led to its emergence? What is its philosophy? These and several other questions related to Dalit literature will be addressed in this chapter.

CASTE AS POWER

As mentioned in the previous chapter, Indian society is fundamentally caste-centric. Therefore the power and privileges available in Indian society are distributed along caste lines. Caste laws were made to prevent Dalits from entering into civic and social spheres of life. Michel Foucault's thesis of knowledge and power can be applied here in order to understand one of the primary ways in which Dalits were oppressed. His premise is that knowledge – its production and dissemination – cannot be separated from the complex activity of domination:

> What makes power hold good, what makes it accepted, is simply the fact that it does not only weigh on us as a force that says no, but that it traverses and produces things, it induces pleasure, forms knowledge, produces discourse. It needs to be considered as a productive network which runs through the whole social body, much more than as negative instance whose function is repression. (119)

This is precisely what happened in caste society. The hegemony of the high castes became so pervasive because all knowledge was generated and processed by them. One of the best examples of this was how learning and using Sanskrit as a language was the privilege of the upper castes. Dalits and women were barred from having access to this language and this was apparently codified in the Vedas, smritis and puranas. Thus, the Sanskrit language, which was the repository of knowledge and wisdom at that time, became a closely guarded terrain where no outsiders were permitted. Some of the immediate effects of this policy were the non-proliferation of Sanskrit and the creation of an outer group, the 'untouchables', whose sole purpose of existence was to serve the interests of the upper-caste people. As a result, for centuries, this community remained permanently at the periphery of society even though they participated in its production process. Ironically, though the people occupying the lowest strata of society were rendered 'untouchables', the goods they produced were somehow deemed acceptable for use.

Curbed under caste rules, the 'untouchables' were allowed only a few avenues through which they could articulate their creative talents. Since reading and writing were not allowed, they could articulate their creative energies only orally, mostly through songs and music. These folk performances were only meant for the 'untouchables' themselves because the upper castes believed that viewing these performances would be 'polluting'. To make the 'untouchable' lives more difficult, caste prohibitions were enforced so rigidly that talented 'untouchable artistes' were forced to forego their cultural heritage and instead were forced to work for their upper-caste masters as virtual slaves. Thus, under caste society 'untouchable' art could not flourish in spite of all its potential.

On the other hand, Indian caste society created conditions for the development of upper-caste art, culture and literature. It was during the Gupta period in ancient India that a 'golden age', when upper-caste artistes invested their time and energy to establish an upper-caste Hindu culture, was facilitated (Majumdar). It was during this time that the poets and playwrights like Kalidasa wrote romantic tales of India from the upper-caste points of view. For example, in the play *Abhijñānashākuntalam* (fourth century CE) Kalidasa gives power and authority to brahmin priests and kshatriya kings, while shudras, ati-shudras and women are mostly silenced. The fisherman, a representative of the lower castes in the play, is depicted as a thief who is jailed just because he finds the signet ring of King Dushyanta in the stomach of a fish. Indian literature is full of such instances where the lower castes, particularly 'untouchables', are depicted as thieves and robbers and, therefore, criminalising them. Since the 'untouchables' had no way to counteract such views, an alternative narrative could not be heard.

It was only during the period of the Bhakti movement (roughly from the eighth to eighteenth centuries) that we got to hear a few untouchable voices, like that of Chokhamela, who broke the shackles of caste and sang their songs of protest in the public domain. Chokhamela was a mahar saint–poet of Maharashtra. Though there is no evidence to suggest that Chokhamela formally protested against the traditional limits of mahar village work, the internal evidence of his *abhangs* suggests some protest against the concept of 'untouchability'. In one of his *abhangs,* Chokhamela writes that he was born as an outcaste mahar because of his past *karma*, while in another *abhang* he addresses God saying,

> Why have you thrown
> this challenge god?
> Solve this riddle of mine;

> enter my shoes, know
> in your own self:
> an outcaste,
> what rights do I enjoy?
> Says Chokha,
> this low born
> human body every
> one drives away.
> Doubts prey
> on my mind,
> what can I do? (Mokashi-Punekar 14)

Even though Chokhamela was a great devotee of Lord Vitthoba, he was not allowed to enter his temple. In fact, there is a story about Chokhamela being severely punished because the priests believed that he had entered the temple at the dead of the night and had stolen the god's golden necklace.

> One day Chokha was standing at the door of the temple from morning till late in the evening, somewhat hopeless and unusually cast down. Towards nightfall, the priests locked up the doors and went away. As Chokha stood there, still and lone, Vitthoba himself came out, exclaimed in distress to see Chokha patiently waiting, embraced him, led him to his breast. The night was spent in the union of the *bhakt* with the God, after which Vitthoba playfully removed his tulsi garland (a garland made of basil seeds which the *varkaris* wear as a mark of their identity) and put it around Chokha's neck. When the day dawned, he led him out of the temple, still with the garland. Chokha, in a state of bliss after this vouchsafing of divine love, lay down on the sands of the river in a trance. At the temple the priests discovered that Vitthoba's gold necklace had disappeared and remembering that Chokha had been at the temple doors last, went into transports of rage over the fact that the temple and deity were polluted and the necklace stolen. Search parties found Chokha still dazed and uncomprehending, but with a gold necklace around the neck. He was punished; tied to the bullocks and about to be dragged to death but for the animals who stood their ground, despite the whip lashing them. The story ends with Vitthoba revealing

> himself to the entire company, holding the bullocks by the horns. (Mokashi-Punekar xv–xvi)

So far as the Bhakti movement is concerned, Chokha was not the only protesting saint–poet against brahminic Hinduism. There were several: the tailor Namdev, the weaver Kabir, the cobbler Ravidas, the cotton comber Dadu Dayal, the potter Gora and the barber Sena, among others. These saint–poets sang songs of liberation in their local languages for the masses; hence, their message spread far and wide. But, overall, the Bhakti movement was local and remained confined to particular linguistic regions because of the lack of translation of their poetry. It took a long time to document and translate these poems from one language to another, including in English.

Apart from rare instances such as these, the 'untouchables' simply remained as outsiders in the cultural and literary productions of Indian caste society. With no platform to articulate their selves, they remained voiceless for a very long time. More significantly, the lack of access to formal education prevented the lower castes from beginning a genuine literary movement that could protest against the monopoly of the established literary canon. That began to slowly change with the advent of the British in India.

ENGLISH EDUCATION IN INDIA

One of the most important events that occurred during British rule was the introduction of English education in schools and colleges in 1835, a result of the now famous Macaulay Minute. With the introduction of English, a new language hierarchy was established among Indians that was largely superimposed upon the existing caste structure. This new opportunity made available by the colonial government was grasped largely by those who were already at the top of the traditional social structure. In other words, people who had earlier studied Sanskrit and Persian now began to avail themselves of the benefits of English education. Thus, caste Hindus who had easy access to higher education in the new dispensation also obtained better jobs in the British administration. Naturally, Dalits, Adivasis, shudras and women could not avail of such opportunities.

However, the different policies introduced by the British government brought about several changes in the social structures of caste society. All through the nineteenth century, the building of roads and railways, the introduction of postal services, the telegraph, the printing press, and many other industries by the British helped India organise itself in new ways through improved communication networks. English language education introduced ideas of Enlightenment which resulted in the incorporation of new secular and democratic ideas into a reformation movement in Indian society. This reform movement, which is also known as the 'Indian Renaissance', attempted in a major way to rid society of its old orthodoxies regarding caste and gender. Women's education, widow remarriage, equality before God, etc., were some of the issues taken up by the leaders in different parts of the country. Yet, strangely enough, in the creative literature of that period the lower castes and the outcastes were virtually invisible. Since education was not available to them, they formed no part of the reader public. And since caste-Hindu life had been organised to keep them at the peripheries, they did not figure in the Indian language novels about social and domestic life that began to be written in the latter half of the nineteenth century.

Education as Emancipation

It was during British rule that 'untouchables' for the first time had the opportunity to avail of formal education in schools, thanks to the efforts of Christian missionaries. They opened their mission schools to the 'untouchables', women and shudras. Probably inspired by Christian missionaries, Jotibarao Phule and his wife Savitribai opened a school especially for 'untouchable' boys and girls. The Phules believed, and rightly so, that education would emancipate the oppressed classes as education had the potential to awaken a kind of consciousness that could finally bring about real change in society. Muktabai, a Dalit girl, studied in one of the schools set up by the Phules in Pune. The eleven-year-old Mukta wrote a fascinating essay in Marathi titled *Mang maharachya dukhvisayi* (About the grief of the mangs and mahars) which was published in

1855 by *Dnyanodaya*, an Ahmednagar-based journal. This essay is, perhaps, the earliest surviving piece of writing by a Dalit woman. In the essay, Mukta openly attacks the way brahminic culture and religion oppress the lower castes, especially the 'untouchables'. She condemns the upper castes saying,

> These people drove us, the poor Mangs and Mahars, away from our own lands, which they occupied to build large buildings. And that was not all. They would make the Mangs and Mahars drink oil mixed with red lead and buried our people in the foundations of their buildings, thus, wiping out generation after generation of our poor people. The Brahmans have degraded us so low; they consider people like us even lower than cows and buffaloes. Did they not consider us even lower than donkeys during the rule of Bajirao Peshwa? . . . Under Bajirao's rule, if any Mang and Mahar happened to pass in front of a gymnasium, they would cut off his head and play "bat and ball" with their swords as bats and his head as a ball, on the grounds. When we were punished for even passing through their doors, where was the question of getting education? (qtd. in Mani and Sardar 72–73)

Muktabai, like the Phules and many other non-brahmin leaders, believed that education would bring freedom to the lower castes. She explains how knowledge will give them power to question the status quo of Indian caste society and eventually bring about a social revolution to the advantage of the 'untouchables'. She writes,

> Oh, the Mahars and Mangs, you are poor and sick. Only the medicine of knowledge will cure and heal you. It will take you away from wild beliefs and superstitions. You will become righteous and moral. It will stop your exploitation. People who treat you like animals will not dare to treat like that anymore. So please work hard and study. Get educated and become good human beings. (75)

Once the 'untouchables' started becoming literate, they began to articulate their protests, concerns and sense of self. But before we discuss Dalit articulation itself, let us try to see whether upper-caste Indian writers were concerned about Dalit lives.

TREATMENT OF CASTE IN EARLY MODERN LITERATURE

At the end of the nineteenth and early parts of the twentieth century many prominent upper-caste Indian writers sporadically took up the cause of the 'untouchables' through their writings. These early writings mostly came from Kerala and Bengal. There are at least three novels from Kerala which deal with issues relating to caste. *Ghatakavadham* (*The Slayer Slain*) was written in 1864–65 by one Mrs Collins, an English missionary, and was published in 1877. The novel is about an 'untouchable' pulaya slave who is ill-treated by his arrogant Syrian Christian landlord. The author ends the novel by emphasising the landlord's change of heart towards the lower-caste slave. Potheri Kunhambu's *Saraswativijayam* (The victory of knowledge) was published in 1892. Hailing from the lower-caste thiyya community, Kunhambu seems to suggest in the novel that conversion to Christianity is the only solution to the lower-caste problem. Kunhambu never became a Christian himself. In the course of the narrative he underlines the need for conversion so that lower-caste people can, at last, avail of education. In the novel, a pulaya slave, after getting severely beaten by his namboodiri (brahmin) landlord, escapes death and becomes a Christian convert. After being educated by the Church, he eventually becomes a judge and presides over the trial of his former landlord and delivers judgement on him. Another such novel is Joseph Muliyil's *Sukumari* which was published in 1897. The novel brings out various debates around whether conversion to Christianity is a right step for the people of the lower castes. Reading all the three novels together, Dilip M. Menon, in his article 'No, Not the Nation: Lower Caste Malayalam Novels of the Nineteenth Century', writes, 'What is significant about early novels is that when not locating themselves in a romantic or historical past, they addressed a troubled present in which questions of self, community and society had to be posed afresh' (Mukherjee 41). The 'troubled present' he talks of is none other than the caste questions posed in all three novels mentioned above.

Unlike Kerala, Bengal did not produce any lower-caste oriented novels during this period. However, there were several discursive essays on caste. For example, Bankim Chandra Chatterjee, a very important Bengali writer, in his essay 'Samya' (Equality), wrote that 'for the oppressed, oppression by high caste countrymen was not less than galling than oppression by arrogant foreigners' (Ghose 216). Yet, not even one of Bankim's fourteen novels deals with the theme of caste oppression, nor are there any characters in his fictional worlds who come from outside caste-Hindu society.

Rabindranath Tagore, another famous Bengali writer, condemns the unjust social order of Indian caste society and seeks justice for the lower castes in his essay *Nationalism*. He writes, 'It was out of the narrowness of sympathy that Indians had denied the inferior castes, their social rights and as long as Indian society remained unjust, there could be no justice in politics' (qtd. in Ghose 215). In at least one famous poem Tagore lashes out at the humiliation meted out to 'untouchables' in our country, predicting that the caste asymmetry will one day drag down the privileged to the same level of degradation:

> O my fortunate country,
> Those whom you have insulted,
> You will have to come down to their level,
> Through insults. (Tagore 72, my translation)

Also, one of his plays, *Chandalika* (1938), deals with the subjectivity of an 'untouchable' girl. In his discursive prose, Tagore often comes back to caste-related problems. Some of his short stories and a few novels, for example *Gora* (1909), deal marginally with his concern about caste injustice, but we do not find a single major character belonging to a low caste of 'untouchable' status in any of his novels. This led Mulk Raj Anand to say in the 1930s that '[m]ost Indian writers of the modern period, like Bankim Chatterjee, Ratan Nath Sarshar and Rabindranath Tagore had not accepted in their novels that even the so-called lowest dregs of humanity, living in utmost poverty, squalor and degradation could become heroes of fiction' (Duggal 3).

At the beginning of the twentieth century, the few upper-caste Hindu writers who attempted to portray the lives of the 'untouchables' tended to be driven either by zeal for social reform or by sentimental compassion. Unnava Lakshminarayana's

Malapalli in Telugu (1921) is supposedly the first Indian language novel where Dalits were portrayed as full-fledged characters. *Malapalli* was followed by Premchand's *Rangbhumi* in Hindi (1925), K. Shivaram Karanth's *Chomana dudi* in Kannada (1933), Mulk Raj Anand's *Untouchable* in English (1935), Thakazhi Sivasankara Pillai's *Thottiyude makan* in Malayalam (1948), Gopinath Mohanty's *Harijan* in Odia (1948), U. R. Ananthamurthy's *Samskara* (1965) and *Bharathipura* in Kannada (1973), and in English, Shanta Rameshwar Rao's *Children of God* (1976), Romen Basu's *Outcast* (1986), Bonomali Goswami's *Untouchables: A Novel* (1994), Rohinton Mistry's *A Fine Balance* (1995), Arundhati Roy's *The God of Small Things* (1997), Manu Joseph's *Serious Men* (2010) and several others where Dalits are the central characters.

But the novels produced by these writers can be termed as 'emotional' literature because these Dalit characters have mostly been imagined from the upper-caste writers' point of view. Therefore, these characters look totally absurd. Rarely did these writers take up any 'untouchable' characters and treat them realistically like ordinary human beings full of vitality, hope as well as despair. Due to space constraints we will only analyse one of these novels as an example of unrealistic portrayal of lower-caste characters. Let us look at Unnava Lakshminarayana's *Malapalli*, one of the earliest non-Dalit novels about Dalits, so that we understand how Dalits as subjects are treated in Indian literature.

Unnava Lakshminarayana's *Malapalli*

Malapalli is considered the first Indian novel that deals with the problems of Dalits in a major way. Written in the aftermath of Gandhi's Non-cooperation Movement in the 1920s, the novel depicts events that take place in the villages of south India during British rule. The protagonists of the novel are mostly the malas of Andhra Pradesh, who are considered 'untouchables' to this day. The central characters – Ramadas, Mahalakshmi, Venkatadas, Sangadas, Jyoti and Appadas – all suffer because of their low-caste status. The novelist seems to suggest at the end that their suffering finally yields fruit. The author finds a solution to their problems through love, rectitude and self-sacrifice.

When the novel begins, we find Ramadas and his family members living in a state of happiness. Ramadas is a small farmer who has ten acres of land. He is hard working and prosperous. Because of his loving nature he serves the needy and the poor whenever he gets the chance. He yearns for knowledge, values piety and honesty, and wants everyone around him – including his family – to imbibe and practice good values. Trouble arises when Ramadas's son Sangadas, with the help and support of his friend Ramanaidu (an educated upper caste), demands proper wages from Choudarayya, the landlord and Ramanaidu's father. Sangadas and Ramanaidu join hands to protect the interests of the workers by mobilising them and go to the extent of calling a hunger strike. Choudarayya, being a cruel landlord, has the upper hand. He is supported by the British administration. During the course of the story, the protestors along with all the members of Ramadas's family end up in jail. For the sake of justice, Venkatadas, Sangadas, Jyoti and Appadas' precious lives are sacrificed.

Finally, it seems that they win their battle. As the author tells us, when Choudarayya wants to take over the property owned by the malas, he loses the case in the court. With this verdict comes liberation for the malas. All the prisoners, including Ramadas, are released from jail. Ramanaidu, being liberal and democratic, has the land registered under a trust which later sets up a college called 'Vijaya College' (in memory of Venkatadas's victory over the caste system). Venkatadas had saved five lakhs to establish an educational institution exclusively for 'untouchables', who had no opportunity to avail of education through government schools and colleges. Thus, finally, Venkatadas's dream comes true. The trust appoints Ramadas as the vice-chancellor of the college. As time passes, the college becomes a centre for the development of the depressed classes.

Unnava Lakshminarayana was a lawyer by profession. Following Gandhi's call during the Non-cooperation Movement, he quit the legal profession and was jailed for his participation in the movement. In fact, the entire novel was written in jail. Gandhi was his ideal. Apart from participating in the freedom movement, he worked whole-heartedly for the upliftment of the poor and downtrodden. It was his belief that in Indian society, everyone, irrespective of caste, class and gender, could reach a higher level given the opportunity. The resolution of the novel is clearly a statement that he believed in and lived throughout his life. He depicts Ramadas, like Gandhi, as an ideal Indian who, after completing all his necessary worldly deeds, withdraws completely from the world to become a sanyasi:

> Ramadas kept his loom in a corner of the college and wove cloth. He made a living with the money that came from the sale proceeds. The sound of the loom could be heard almost all the time. He wore saffron clothes all the time and shone like the setting sun with the radiance of the Creator. He would go up the hill almost every day and sometimes he would even sleep there. After a while he stopped coming to the college or into the village. No one knew where he had gone. The elders said that he had gone into the caves in the hill as a *Siddha,* Accomplished One, and in due course had become one with the Creator. (382)

This is typical of an upper-caste writer who believes in Indian tradition and tries to implement his project of Indian *dharma* and *karma* through his 'untouchable' characters. This is clearly evident when Ramadas finally renounces the very world which he has tried to build for the betterment of both 'touchables' and 'untouchables'. The author was a staunch follower of Gandhian ideals and his validation of the Gandhian project is unmistakable. Although, at times, Gandhi was critical of the Indian tradition, he was a votary of several traditional customs and practices, including *varnashrama dharma*. According to Gandhi, *varnashrama dharma* was a simple division of labour, which would help India prosper if people followed it earnestly. He also justified it saying that its main function was to avoid competition among different caste constituencies so that peace and harmony prevailed in society. This argument of Gandhi's was later contested by Ambedkar who felt that caste needed to be annihilated in order for the lower castes to attain dignity and self-respect. As Ambedkar argued, *varnashrama dharma* as a social system does not allow people from the lower castes to choose a profession. But Lakshminarayana, being an ardent follower of Gandhi, was uncritical of Gandhi's ideals. Therefore, he brings many of the Hindu discourses that Gandhi endorsed into his novel.

However, it may also be noted that *Malapalli* was much ahead of its time in its choice of Dalit issues as its central theme. By the time Lakshminarayana wrote the novel, Gandhi had just started his campaign for India's freedom struggle as a leader of the Non-cooperation Movement. At this time Gandhi had not taken up any major programme relating to untouchability though he had already condemned its practice in Indian society. For example, in his article in *Young India* on 15 January 1921 he wrote,

> Has not a just nemesis overtaken us for the crime of untouchability? Have we not reaped as we have sown? Have we not practised Dyerism or O'Dwyerism on our kith and kin? We have segregated the *pariah* and we are in turn segregated in the British colonies. We deny him the use of public wells; we throw the leavings of our plates at him. His very shadow pollutes us. Indeed there is no charge that the *pariah* cannot fling in our face which we do not fling in the faces of Englishmen. (qtd. in Bhattacharya and Rao 69)

It was at Gandhi's insistence that the Congress took up the cause of 'untouchables' as part of its social welfare programme. However, it was only in 1932, in the aftermath of the Poona Pact with Ambedkar, that Gandhi started his 'Harijan' movement on a large scale. In fact, one of the major agendas of the movement was the issue of Dalits not being able to enter temples or places of worship. It was, therefore, a mark of progressive thinking on the part of Lakshminarayana to have taken up issues relating to 'untouchables' in 1921. By making 'untouchables' the protagonists of his novel he did the Dalit constituency a great service.

This trend, which started with Lakshminarayana in 1921, has continued, as the novels produced by upper-caste Indian writers from Shivaram Karanth to Manu Joseph suggest. There is no doubt that their writings show their involvement with the underprivileged and the dispossessed. Yet, in spite of being progressive, these writers, by virtue of their birth and education, stood outside the arena of suffering endured by the 'untouchables' and other underprivileged classes. Naturally, the representation of the poor and the downtrodden in their works was bound to be different from the self-representation of Dalits – a trend which began in the post-independence era.

DALIT ARTICULATIONS IN THE EARLY TWENTIETH CENTURY

Prior to India's independence, and even before Gandhi and Ambedkar had launched their movements on caste and untouchability, a Dalit poet named Hira Dom from the Central Provinces published a poem titled *Achhut ki shikayat* (An untouchable's complaint) in the September 1914 issue of the Hindi magazine, *Saraswati*. This is one of the first published pieces of Dalit writing and certainly the earliest example of Dalit writing in Hindi. In his long poem, Hira Dom draws attention to the double discrimination faced by the 'untouchables' from both the colonial administration and the upper castes. Toral Jatin Gajarawala, a literary critic, in *Untouchable Fictions*, traces the genealogy of Dalit literature in Hira Dom's poem:

> Wielding a two-pronged critique against both the upper castes and their colonial rulers, Hira Dom concludes with a plea for mutual fraternity among castes, drawing on the language of national republicanism. Although that sentiment requires another sixty-five years of caste radicalism and the bureaucratic engines of independence, constitutional protection, and education to produce what we now recognize as Dalit literature, the timing is more than coincidental. (33)

Less than a year later, Mohini Chamarin, a Dalit woman from the same province as Hira Dom, published a short story, *Chhot ke chor* (Thieves of the subordinated) in the August 1915 volume of a Hindi magazine named *Kanya Manoranjan*. Mohini's story, like Hira Dom's poem, would not have had much impact on the Hindi reading public. Thanks to recent interest by scholars in Dalit writing, the lost literature of the past is now being retrieved and read with care. Charu Gupta, a historian, believes that Mohini, being a Dalit woman, is automatically a victim of not just caste but also of a patriarchal social order. Gupta observes,

> Probably one of the first stories in Hindi by a Dalit woman to get into print – in a region where the illiteracy rates of Chamar

> women were as high as 99.99 per cent – this was indeed a remarkable feat. Mohini Chamarin and her story, however, have been lost in the pages of history. Not only was the Dalit print-public-sphere in colonial India largely coded as male, even its later narratives have been overwhelmingly male-centric. (267)

Gupta's observation seems valid because the upper-caste reading public always tried to ignore the protesting voices of the oppressed as they challenged their hegemonic power. This is something that Dalit academics and researchers have been able to prove recently. For example, while tracing the history of Telugu Dalit literature one can consider the *Jambava puranam* of the madigas and the *Chenna puranam* of the malas (rediscovered in the nineteenth century) as early examples of Dalit articulation. In fact, between ancient and modern times, there are many Telugu Dalit voices, mostly poets, who have recorded their protests against the monopoly of caste. One such poet was Bhagya Reddy, who wrote in 1934,

> We are seven crore people, beware!
> We are now empowered . . .
> the stream of reform flows swiftly in favour of the Scheduled
> Castes.
> Who can swim against the tide?
> You should adjust yourself like the reeds do in swift currents,
> or else you will find it difficult. (Purushotham et al. xv)

Reddy wrote this poem in the aftermath of the Poona Pact of 1932, when the social reform movements undertaken by both Ambedkar and Gandhi were in full swing. Seven years after Reddy's poem, in 1941, Gurram Jashuva wrote *Gabbilam* (*Bat*) which subsequently became an important milestone publication in modern Telugu Dalit poetry. Jashuva's character in the poem is a poor untouchable madiga who earns his livelihood by making and mending sandals. He sends a message to god through a bat which resides in the temple premises. Jashuva portrays his untouchable character thus:

> He is innocent, so he is happy
> with what little he earns.
> He is hungry, so he forgets his cares
> if he has a meal.

He lives in a space with only
the four directions to protect him.
He is an untouchable,
the last-born son
of India that is Bharat. (Purushotham et al. 27)

Jashuva's Dalit consciousness strikes at the centre of Hinduism which subscribes to the *dharma* and *karma* theory and divides caste occupations accordingly. The poet strongly interrogates such Hindu beliefs in the following words:

They shut my mouth
with their karma theory
and steal my food from me.
What was my karma? (29)

It may be significant to emphasise here that neither the writing of Hira Dom nor Jashuva's poem was available to a larger reading public because they were not available in translation, either in English or in any other Indian language. It is only after 1991–92, coincident with the birth centenary of Ambedkar, that Dalit writing began to be translated in English and became available to the English-reading public in India and abroad. Arjun Dangle's *Poisoned Bread: Translations from Modern Marathi Dalit Literature* (1992) was the first edited anthology of Dalit writing to come out in English. This was followed by several such anthologies of Dalit writings both in English translations as well as in Indian languages. (The politics of translation and Dalit writing is an issue which we will explore in the next chapter.)

THE DALIT LITERARY MOVEMENT

In post-independence India, educated Dalits who had tasted the fruits of modern education realised the need for an alternative mode of thinking and launched a new literary movement. It is no surprise that the movement started in Maharashtra, the homeland of Ambedkar. It is important to recall here that Ambedkar had established the People's Society in Bombay in 1945 and started Siddharth College, hoping that education would open new avenues for Dalits. His famous call, 'educate, unite and agitate', was being spiritedly followed by the Dalit masses.

Around 1950, when the first batch of Dalit youths graduated from Siddharth College, Ghanashyam Talwatkar and others set up a literary society called the Siddharth Sahitya Sangh. This was later renamed the Maharashtra Dalit Sahitya Sangh. Dalit writers and activists had planned to have the first Dalit writers' conference in December 1956, which was to be inaugurated by Ambedkar. Unfortunately, Ambedkar passed away on 6 December 1956. His passing away was a big jolt for the Dalit movement, and it took a while for Dalit writers and activists to come together to take his movement forward. The first conference of Dalit writers was then organised in Bombay in 1958. The inaugural speech was delivered by eminent Dalit writer Anna Bhau Sathe. In his speech he clearly spelt out the purpose of Dalit literature, emphasising its social responsibility. Dalit writers and activists who attended the conference resolved to bring their writing under the banner of Dalit literature. For example, 'Resolution No. 5' of the conference says, 'That the literature written by the Dalits and that written by others about the Dalits in Marathi be accepted as a separate entity known as "Dalit literature" and realizing its cultural importance, the universities and literary organizations should give it its proper place'. This resolution was published in volume 4, number 3 of *Prabuddha Bharat* in 1958 (Dangle 242).

This first conference of Dalit writers in Maharashtra went almost unnoticed by the upper-caste intelligentsia. There were also differences and factions that arose among Dalit activists, writers and politicians who attended the conference and thereafter. There were also differences over what name was to be given to this new literature. Some called it Dalit literature while others used terms such as Ambedkarite literature, Gramin literature, Buddhist literature, and so on. It took time for the Dalit youths to come together under a common umbrella while setting aside the factionalism that had arisen within the literary movement. This was the start of the Dalit Panthers movement. Namdeo Dhasal, Arjun Dangle and J. V. Pawar established the Dalit Panthers in Bombay on 9 July 1972. That year the Panthers observed the silver jubilee of India's Independence

Day as Black Day, and held black-flag demonstrations at various places in Bombay. Dangle recollects how it was a unique literary movement:

> Dalit Panthers came to be established through the Dalit literary movement. The leaders of the Dalit Panthers were all writers. A wave of literature expressing one's experience in provocative language swept over Marathi literature. Maharashtra was again charged with discussions on Dalit literature and language. This was probably the first time in India that creative writers became politically active and led a movement. (254)

The main objective of this movement was to create a counterculture and create a distinct/separate identity for Dalits in society. The Panthers' call for social reconstruction was further activised by Dalit writers and poets through various forms of writing and speeches. Thus, modern Dalit literature emerged in Maharashtra in the early 1970s and subsequently spread to the neighbouring states of Gujarat and Karnataka, a phenomenon which later launched literary movements all over India.

The Dalit youths of Gujarat were heavily influenced by the work of the Dalit Panthers. On the occasion of Ambedkar's birth anniversary in 1974, they invited Raja Dhale, J. V. Pawar and Bhai Sangare, leaders of the Dalit Panthers, to Ahmedabad and organised several meetings to promote the Dalit Panthers ideology. Among others, Naginbhai Parmar, Dalpat Shrimali, Valjibhai Patel, Bakul Vakil and P. D. Vaghela were the prominent organisers of this event. This resulted in the rise of a strong Dalit literary and cultural movement in Gujarat. Influenced by the Dalit Panthers of Maharashtra, Dalit poets and writers like Dalpat Chauhan, Pravin Gadhvi, Nirav Patel and others began experimenting with the theme of caste oppression and class exploitation in their writings. The initiative taken by these three poets took a new turn in 1975 when several educated Dalit writers and activists of Gujarat gathered in Ahmedabad to give a proper shape to the emerging Dalit consciousness in the state. They decided to start a monthly magazine titled *Panther* in order to carve out a creative space of their own. Many Dalit poets and writers had their writing published through this magazine. Encouraged by the growth of a reading public, several Dalit poetry collections came out during the early part of 1980s. For example, in 1981 *Dalit Kavita*, an anthology of poetry, was edited by Ganpat Parmar and Manishi Jani. Chandu Maheria and Balkrishna Anand edited another collection of poetry titled *Visphot* in 1982. Chandu Maheria edited *Asmita* in 1983.These anthologies are the work of individual poets and writers who made concerted efforts to draw the attention of the readers to a new kind of writing that was coming from the margins.

By the 1980s the upper castes of Gujarat had already taken a note of the Dalit collective. Afraid that educated Dalits would slowly take over every sector of public life, the upper castes vehemently opposed the reservation policy and organised a series of attacks on the Dalit population – first in 1981 and then in 1985. These two events led the Dalits of Gujarat to unite across communities. Educated Dalits began to deconstruct their pasts in order to express their feeling of alienation and to search for their identities. They began articulating a new Dalit discourse and incorporated it into various subjects – be it Dalit history, Dalit sociology, Dalit art, or Dalit literature. Today, Gujarat, like Maharashtra, has a rich Dalit literature tradition to showcase.

Karnataka too developed a healthy Dalit literary movement very early. In a function held on 19 November 1973, organised by the Dr Ambedkar Vichara Vedike and the Backward Class Students Forum of the University of Mysore, B. Basavalingappa, a Dalit minister in the Devraj Urs government, delivered a speech titled 'Kannada literature as *bhusa* (cattle feed) literature'. This led to widespread public protests in the state, and the birth of 'Bandaya Sahitya', similar to Dalit literature. A spate of literary magazines such as *Dalitha*, *Panchama*, *Andolana*, *Shudra* and *Sankramana* came out. The Dalit movement in Karnataka eventually led to the formation of the Dalit Sangharsh Samiti in June 1977. Devanoor Mahadeva, Siddalingaiah, Devaiah Harave, B. Krishnappa, K. Ramaiah, Indudhara Honnapura, Manchaiah, Govindaiah and many other Dalit writers and activists played an important role in the formation of the Samiti. Karnataka now has a vibrant Dalit movement and a rich corpus of Dalit literature.

Dalit literature in other states came to be established gradually. By the 1990s, Dalit literature was available in almost all Indian languages. The Mandal Commission recommendations and Ambedkar's birth centenary empowered Dalits to emphatically assert their position vis-à-vis caste powers. These two events brought caste debates back into the public imagination. In 1991–92, when the V. P. Singh government celebrated Ambedkar's birth centenary, 'equity with social justice' was the catchphrase heard everywhere. In the same year, the Department of Education of the Government of Maharashtra brought out twenty volumes of the writings and speeches of Ambedkar in English, edited by Vasant Moon (*Dr Babasaheb Ambedkar: Writings and Speeches*). These volumes were later translated into all Indian languages. With Ambedkar's ideology spreading all over India, a pan-Indian Dalit consciousness came into existence.

CONCLUSION

The emergence of Dalit literature was an outcome of Dalit movements and symbolised the coming of a new vocal community. Dalit writing can be understood as a voicing of the hopes and aspirations of a group of people who were earlier nameless, faceless and voiceless under the caste system, who were now able to speak and assert their identities as new political subjects. Their fight for human dignity and self-respect, in the meantime, has given them a new vocabulary through which they are writing their own stories and histories. Dalit writers are, thus, writing a revolution, keeping in mind a new, egalitarian democracy which will be casteless and classless. As K. Satyanarayana and Susie Tharu emphasise, 'They are critiquing and rearranging the field of dominant culture and the politics of the upper castes by unsettling the boundaries, frames, figures and ideologies' (65). In this egalitarian project, what exactly is the role of a Dalit writer? How can Dalit literature achieve this goal? To understand these questions, we will look into the various aspects of Dalit aesthetics in our next chapter.

REFERENCES

Anand, Mulk Raj. *Untouchable*. New Delhi: Arnold Associates, 1981, 1935. Print.

Basu, Romen. *Outcast.* New Delhi: Sterling Publishers, 1986. Print.

Bhattacharya, Sabyasachi, and Yagati Chinna Rao. *The Past of the Outcaste: Readings in Dalit History*. Hyderabad: Orient BlackSwan, 2017. Print.

Dangle, Arjun, ed. *Poisoned Bread: Translations from Modern Marathi Dalit Literature*. Bombay: Orient Longman, 1994. Print.

Duggal, K. S, ed. *Writer in Freedom Struggle*. Chandigarh: Twenty-first Century Indian Society, 1988. Print.

Foucault, Michael. *Power/Knowledge*. Ed. Paul Rabinow. New York: Peregrine Books, 1984. Print.

Gajarawala, Toral Jatin. *Untouchable Fictions: Literary Realism and the Crisis of Caste*. New York: Fordham UP, 2013. Print.

Ghose, Shankar. *The Western Impact on Indian Politics*. New Delhi: Allied Publishers, 1967. Print.

Goswami, Bonomali. *Untouchables: A Novel*. New Delhi: Mittal Publications, 1994. Print.

Gupta, Charu. *The Gender of Caste: Representing Dalits in Print*. Ranikhet: Permanent Black, 2016. Print.

Kalidasa. *The Abhijñānashākuntalam of Kalidasa*. Trans. M. R. Kale. Delhi: Motilal Banarsidas, 2010. Print.

Lakshminarayana, Unnava. *Malapalli*. Trans. V. V. B. Rama Rao. New Delhi: Sahitya Akademi, 2008. Print.

Majumdar, R. C. *Ancient India*. Delhi: Motilal Banarsidass Publishers, 1994. Print.

Mani, Braj Ranjan, and Pamela Sardar. *A Forgotten Liberator: The Life and Struggle of Savitribai Phule*. New Delhi: Mountain Peak, 2010. Print.

Mokashi-Punekar, Rohini. *On the Threshold: Songs of Chokhamela*. New Delhi: The Book Review Literary Trust, 2002. Print.

Mukherjee, Meenakshi, ed. *Early Novels in India*. New Delhi: Sahitya Akademi, 2010. Print.

Purushotham, K., et al., eds. *The Oxford India Anthology of Telugu Dalit Writing*. New Delhi: Oxford UP, 2016. Print.

Satyanarayana, K., and Susie Tharu, ed. *No Alphabet in Sight: New Dalit Writing from South India*. New Delhi: Penguin Books, 2011. Print.

Tagore, Rabindranath. *Rabindra Rachanabali*. Volume 7. Santiniketan: Viswabharati, 1986. Print.

Chapter Four

Understanding Dalit Aesthetics

As discussed in the previous chapter, Indian literature, as a whole, does not seem to have done any justice to the question of caste or Dalit communities. Even a cursory look at Indian literature written in any of the Indian languages or in English suggests that the idea of caste has not only been misread but misrepresented. However, the emergence of Dalit literature has led to fresh debates around the representation of caste, class, ethnicity, language, region, nationalism, religion and gender. By initiating discussions on these issues, Dalit writers have started challenging the dominant assumptions of the traditional elites who have controlled knowledge systems in India. They are also rewriting India's histories from the perspective of oppressed Indians. Toral Jatin Gajarawala describes this project:

> Dalit literature might be broadly read as a corrective to a body of work determined to claim nationally representative cultural status. By asserting not only the use of the vernacular, but the deconstruction of class/caste (and gender) and the formal tropes of a broadly conceived modernism, its presence, in addition to its declaration of a certain analytics, serves as a critique of the Indian literary canon as it is generally understood. (166)

Gajarawala's observations underline the way Dalit literature has opened up new avenues to understand Indian society, culture and literature. The way Dalit writers are raising questions around caste, class and gender – among other themes – has never been done before and so openly. The coming of Dalit literature has diversified the category called Indian literature. With its raw and everyday language of the oppressed, Dalit literature has been raising its voice against the hegemonic forces that have appropriated all sorts of resources – social, cultural, economic or religious – for centuries. Dalit literature has already started destabilising power centres and rewriting Indian history, culture, aesthetics and philosophy in a major way. This makes Dalit literature an important force to reckon with. Alok Mukherjee, in his translator's introduction to Sharankumar Limbale's *Towards an Aesthetic of Dalit Literature* (2004), observes,

> Dalits are an important political and social force in India. Their literary and critical writings constitute a major challenge to, and questioning of, the theorizing about Indian politics, society, culture and literature by intellectuals from upper caste Hindu and other dominant communities, and by non-Indians. To fail to pay attention to this challenge and questioning, is to engage in a hegemonic discourse that excludes the realities and experiences of nearly a quarter of the country's people. (Limbale vii–viii)

What is important to note at this juncture is that Dalit literature has emerged as a new area of study, and indeed is part of curricula not just in India, but all over the world. Since Dalit lives are marked by caste as well as class battles, the usage of social realism as a trope puts Dalit writing into a distinctive category. This is a positive development so far as Dalit literature is concerned. But there are still several issues which are yet to be addressed by literary critics and historians. For example, what is the philosophy of Dalit literature? What exactly is Dalit aesthetics? How is it different from Indian aesthetics? How do we understand Dalit language? What is our approach to Dalit literary forms? In other words, how do we read and interpret Dalit texts – those written in English as well as in several Indian languages? We will make an attempt to answer these questions in the following sections.

CONTEXTUALISING DALIT LITERATURE

Since the 1970s, an increasing number of poets and writers from Dalit communities in various Indian states have been producing literary works such as poems, short stories, novels, dramas and autobiographies, representing the themes of caste oppression, untouchability, poverty, repression and revolution. These are broad themes which accommodate many other thematic categories Dalit writers are concerned with. But since caste is the primary target, Dalit writing constitutes a powerful denunciation of and a fierce attack on the caste system and brahminical Hinduism. The dream of every Dalit writer is a casteless society. This egalitarian project of Dalit writers is sometime misunderstood by upper-caste critics. For example, Debjani Ganguly in her book *Caste and Dalit Lifeworlds* (2008), while showing her sympathy for Dalit pain, undertakes a postcolonial reading of caste by emphasising its materiality. The following passage clearly suggests how Dalit pain is pushed to the background by such a reading of caste:

> My attempt to read caste as discourse does not automatically connote a disavowal of the materiality of caste, a disavowal of the way in which its imbrications in South Asian institutional structures affects the lived reality of the people. The pain of the dalit is palpable and embodied. I cannot presume to reduce it to a text or even to a series of texts, or even to discourse pure and simple. Its corporeal presence will forever cast an anguished shadow over anything one writes, or has written, about it. At the same time, it is also a pain that has long, complex and overlapping histories, histories about which there is even today hardly any consensus, notwithstanding the tomes that have been devoted to their analysis. (10)

The corpus of Dalit writing in Indian languages is clearly suggestive of how Dalit writers counter the 'anguished shadow' that Ganguly, a literary and cultural historian, referred to. It is quite unfortunate that while writing about Dalit lives upper-caste literary critics and social scientists, though they empathise with Dalit suffering, highlight only their 'pain'. And to alleviate that 'pain', what they often suggest is the material benefits Dalits should get from both the state and society. Such a superficial reading of caste becomes problematic because material benefits alone will never resolve the everyday problems of Dalits. The Dalit demand is for dignity, self-respect and the right to be treated as human beings, not simply material wealth.

Upper-caste critics often read 'caste' as 'class' and sometimes conflate the two. Therefore, they fail to see the many other things Dalit lifeworlds can offer – be it cultural tropes, religion/spirituality or philosophy, to mention a few – other than the pain arising out of caste and class exploitation. These critics also forget that the primary aim of the Dalit movement is to fight for human dignity along with equity and social justice. Dalit writers emphatically and repeatedly raise questions around these issues.

The state's response to Dalit problems is constructed on premises similar to those of upper-caste critics. People in positions of authority and power think that centuries of injustice can be compensated for through material entitlements. A cultural critic, D. R. Nagaraj argues that the state's response to Dalit issues is inherently flawed because instead of addressing human issues the authorities try to combine a varied agenda comprising dignity, religiosity and material entitlement. Nagaraj comments,

> I cannot agree with the ideologically perceived and politically posited unity between the realms of dignity, religiosity, and entitlements. Historically, this unity is wrong, it dispirits cultural imagination, it is politically self-defeating and short-sighted. Further, a certain notion of power and authority operates behind such a Unitarian vision wherein temporal structures are considered absolute, and material being is considered the only state of authentic experience. If Dalit literature is conceived as an authentic celebration of defiance, a transgression of fatalist modes of existence, then how can it accept a theory of the primacy of the above-said unity? To understand this story of acceptance and the subsequent rebellion, one has to offer a critique of the construction of the caste system and the sources of rebellion against it in the social thought of modern India. In other words, we need to re-create the contours of Dalit imagination by mapping the terrain of the Brahmin mind. (187–88)

Nagaraj is right in saying that the brahmin mind always defended the caste hierarchy which oppressed Dalits to the utmost. Dalit imagination, therefore, has to go deeper to that level where caste as a social system is not just critiqued but where it offers an alternative vision. It is in this context that Dalit writing is seen as an alternative reading to caste ideology. It has been pointed out that Dalit literature is considered to be a unique genre of modern Indian literature as former untouchables themselves are using the traditionally denied weapon of literacy to expose the conditions under which they have lived, as well as to directly rebel against (Hindu) institutions which have subordinated them to the *varna* order. Dalit writers are, in many ways, exposing the deficiencies of the upper-caste writers and reformers who sympathetically viewed Dalit problems and attacked the caste system. Sisir Kumar Das, a literary critic of repute, forcefully makes this point:

> Scholars defending the system always argued that the caste system in its original form was not hereditary, but based on psychological foundation, the division of society according to different groups was in fact an exercise towards the recognition of the innate psychological inclinations of men. Some of them agreed that the complete stratification of the society, denying the lower groups any opportunity towards vertical mobility, was unjust and inhuman. And some condemned it severely. But all writings on caste inequality failed to create any significant impact until the movement against the system emerged from the oppressed themselves. (150–51)

Das is right because until the emergence of Dalit literature, caste-related issues were superficially discussed by upper-caste writers and reformers in the public sphere without deeply understanding the victims' points of view. Therefore in upper-caste writing, Dalits are always depicted as victims and rarely as fighters. Dalit writers, by exposing those lacunae, are also rewriting India's history. S. Sreenivasan, in his article 'Why Does Dalit Literature Matter?', emphasises this point:

> The Dalit experience with its grinding poverty, forced illiteracy, economic exploitation, caste-based social taboos and unending denial of human rights is something which only the Dalits know from the inside. Those who are outside the fold can imagine, sympathise or write about, but they cannot feel the sting, the pain and the humiliation in the way a Dalit feels it. Dalit literature thus articulates experiences to which Dalits alone have access as a matter of historical compulsions. Dalit literature is the insider's report of Dalit experiences, memoir,

> recollections, rebellion rendered in a forthright, imaginative, often predominantly colloquial style. (25)

Sreenivasan's view is important because it foregrounds the fact that Dalit narratives are not just the narratives of pain. They are also documents of lived experiences of Dalits who suffer because of inhuman caste practices. Their explosive narratives, which are full of anger and anguish, therefore need to be historically situated so that we can try to understand the Dalit language of anger and rebellion. In order to understand the location of Dalits in Indian society, culture and literature, we not only need theory, but also history.

DALIT AESTHETICS

Dalit literature has arisen from cultural conflict. Since the 'downtrodden' have hardly any place in the established canonical literature of India, Dalit writers tend to call the existing canon 'Hindu literature' and seek to challenge its hegemony. In the words of Baburao Bagul, a Marathi Dalit writer, 'The established literature of India is Hindu literature. But it is Dalit literature which has the revolutionary power to accept new science and technology and bring about a total transformation. "Dalit" is the name of total revolution; it is revolution incarnate' (Dangle 289).

The Dalit idea of revolution is to bring about a social transformation in India whereby equality and social justice will be available to everyone, including the poor and downtrodden. Dalit writers write about this revolution convincingly, unlike their upper-caste counterparts who often subscribe to the view of either maintaining the status quo or expect a 'change of heart' among the power brokers. We have already seen how the latter view is given voice while discussing Unnava Lakshminarayana's Telugu novel, *Malapalli,* in the previous chapter.

The debate as to who can be called a Dalit writer continues to be a subject of Indian literary criticism. Is a Dalit writer one who belongs to a Dalit community or anyone who writes about the life of Dalits? Caste Hindu writers' work on Dalits has been strongly criticised by Dalit writers for their superficiality of feeling, experiences and interests vis-á-vis Dalits. Even the most progressive and revolutionary writers like Premchand, Mulk Raj Anand, T. S. Pillai, V. S. Khandekar, and several others who have tried to describe the sentiments of Dalits, are not accepted as Dalit writers because of their lack of authenticity. According to many Dalit writers, only a Dalit by birth can have the sensitivity and experience to be a genuine Dalit writer. Dalit writing has been described by Tarachand Khandekar as 'letters of their own blood' (6). They are a natural outburst of the feelings and thoughts that have been denied expression for a long time. On the other hand, non-Dalit writers use idioms and phrases that portray Dalit characters as either fuming at their social position or as accepting the status quo as god-given. Such characterisations cannot validate the lifeworlds of Dalits, writes D. R. Nagaraj: 'Usually anger, pity, and melancholy are the dominant feelings in the literature on Dalits written by non-Dalits. Many a time even the value system of the Dalit world is interpreted wrongly. In creative writings such babysitting for other groups and classes is very awkward' (61).

Dalit writers attempt to be true to their lived experiences and feel that their visions and responses must be translated into art honestly, in its raw, undistilled form without using euphemisms. Their vehicle is often the brutal, coarse and crude language of the slum and village, springing from a life of poverty, ignorance and violence.

> The jaggedness of word, the granulated structure, the rough hewn expression, the scarcely muted anger – anger which may spit fire like wrath, burn lambently like satire, scorch like cynicism, kindle like anguish and enflame like tragedy – these are some of the allotropic forms which are found in the works of Dalit writers in their various works of poetry and prose, fiction and autobiography, drama and essay. (Kumar 148)

There is even an attempt on their part to evolve a new aesthetics because they feel that the genteel expressions of the existing elite literary standards cannot do justice to the quality of life they know and write about.

The different viewpoints of Dalit and non-Dalit writers have also been the subject of scrutiny among academics. One such relevant study is by Joshil K. Abraham and Judith Misrahi-Barak who, in their joint introduction to *Dalit Literatures in India*, write,

> Dalit and non-Dalit writers, thinkers, critics and academics have sometimes been ensnared in possibly inevitable internal debates about the origin of Dalit literature, about its status, and the ways it should be approached. The scope and impact of the literatures themselves may consequently not have been as far-reaching as they should have been. It would be more fruitful to push these debates into the background, widen the contours of these literatures without losing their specificities and write yet unwritten histories of Dalit literatures that have so far been unimaginable in the dominant discourse. (12)

One cannot agree more with Abraham and Misrahi-Barak's point of view because several features of Dalit literature are yet to be properly theorised in a manner that can allow many of its contexts to be properly understood by readers. Foregrounding this view, we can attempt to interpret various features of Dalit literature in a more nuanced way.

Dalit literature, apart from trying to negate caste inequalities and injustices, has a more ambitious project in mind: to bring marginal voices to the centre. This is definitely an uphill task and to some extent, Dalit writers have been successful in their efforts.

Dalit literature denies a majoritarian Hindu mentality and affirms freedom. But this has not gone down well with non-Dalit critics. Dalit literature has been criticised for its forms, structures and languages not being 'literary' in a real sense of the term. Dalit writers and critics, on the other hand, refute these charges saying that Dalit aesthetics is unique in itself because Dalit literature is all about the representation of Dalit life in a realistic mode.

Since Dalits are located at the periphery of Indian caste society, a major preoccupation of Dalit literature is the social location of Dalits. Once referred to as 'untouchables' in Indian society, Dalit writers' works are social narratives of the marginal self which has been a victim of the caste order. Till we become aware of their sociological position, we may not be able to understand the central arguments of Dalit writing. Thus, to evaluate such writing we need a new literary yardstick because the old way of measuring literary standards may not do it justice. Sharankumar Limbale writes,

> The act of imagination called art is impermanent and ever-changing. Unless the yardsticks change, the relationship between literature and criticism will be fractured. In India, there are tremendous differences in levels and processes of taste. What is tasteful to one person may not appear so to another. In these circumstances, it will be wrong to insist on fixed standards. Like literature, criticism, too, is apt to change. Just as the course of literature has changed from one period to another, so has the mode of criticism. To assert that someone's writing will be called literature only when "our" literary standards can be imposed on it is a sign of cultural dictatorship. The yardsticks of literature do not remain standstill for all time. With changing times, literature changes, and there remains the possibility of change in its criticism too. New literary trends cannot be evaluated with traditional literary yardsticks. (107)

It should be said here that the major differences between Dalit and non-Dalit writers are their approach to life and art. Generally speaking, Indian upper-caste writers mainly celebrate beauty through their art. If the *rasa* and *dhwani* theories are any indicators, it is the prerogative of the *rasikas*, lovers of art, to derive pleasure through art and appreciate it. This is the central argument so far as Indian aesthetics is concerned. Literature, being an art form, has to follow this principle. Indian literature, from classical Sanskrit literature to the early twentieth century, more or less followed such principles. It is only after the emergence of progressive writing in the 1930s that literature became a vehicle for social change. Progressive writers like Premchand have raised this point both in their discursive writings as well as fictional accounts. But the problem with most of the progressive writers is that in order to bring about a revolution in Indian society, they often romanticised the characters, locations and events they wrote about. Premchand's depiction of Indian villages and the rural poor, Mulk Raj Anand's Baka-like Dalit characters, U. R. Ananthamurthy's Chandri and Belli as Dalit prostitutes or

Mahasweta Devi's innocent Dalit, tribal and peasant characters are but a few examples of such romanticisation that we often encounter in Indian literature. Compared to upper-caste progressive writers, Dalit writers realistically portray their lives, environment and situations. This truth-telling is necessary for Dalit writers. This is how they speak truth to power.

They also believe that art must be used for the welfare of the masses. Dalit literature, as Omprakash Valmiki in *Dalit sahitya ka saundarya shastra* (The aesthetics of dalit literature) writes, 'is not art for art's sake; it is literature of life and literature of the desire to live' (14, my translation). This is important because it is also a Dalit theorisation of Dalit aesthetics that challenges the way upper-caste writers and theoreticians have understood and propagated Indian aesthetics. It also interrogates the notion of literature and particularly the way the Indian upper-caste writers propagate their worldviews through their art. In this context, Limbale observes,

> The literature of the exploited is primarily concerned with the search for freedom, and giving expression to it. All aspects and dimensions of freedom are seen in it. We should remember that the imaginary or idea of freedom has an aesthetic aspect, as much as it has political, economic, social and moral facets. The sentiment of freedom is present in Dalit literature not only as its life essence, but also as beauty. The three values of life – equality, freedom and solidarity – can be regarded as constituting the essence of beauty in Dalit literature. The aesthetics of Dalit literature rests on: first, the artists' social commitment; second, the life-affirming values present in the artistic creation; and third, the ability to raise the reader's consciousness of fundamental values like equality, freedom, justice and fraternity. (20)

Apart from combining aesthetics with the political, Dalit writers have also been trying to experiment with different literary forms – be it the novel, autobiography or even poetry – to their advantage. Their use of coarse and everyday language is definitely a challenge to non-Dalit readers who are not habituated to the use of such language and dialects in literary texts.

IMPORTANT GENRES IN DALIT LITERATURE

Interestingly, many contributors to Dalit literature are poets. In fact, in the early phase of Dalit writing poetry became the dominant form. The orality of poetry seems to provide the perfect vehicle to convey the distressed utterances of those who have laboured to live and who have been subjugated for so long. One can take any Dalit poem and feel the rhythm of distress arising out of it. This leads E. V. Ramakrishnan, an eminent Indian poet and critic, to say that the collective voice of Dalit communities is found in almost any Dalit poem written in any Indian language. In his book *Making It New: Modernism in Malayalam, Marathi and Hindi Poetry* (1995) Ramakrishnan observes,

> The multi-voicedness that is central to the dialogical approach manifests itself in the Dalit poetry as a dramatic encounter between the collective voice of a community and the members of the same community or those who oppress them. The lyric as a form is not often favoured by these writers because even when the speaking voice is that of an individual, their poetry endeavours to capture the social imagination of the community. (100)

Ramakrishnan is right in his observation because in the multitude of voices in Dalit writing one can always find a dialogic approach to Dalit issues. Since the Dalit project to annihilate caste is a collective endeavour of both Dalits and non-Dalits, Dalit poets and writers have to constantly initiate a dialogue between different constituencies and agencies in society. Secondly, the lyrical form is not really favoured by Dalit poets because the language of revolution is always instant and spontaneous. To write a lyrical poem the poet has to choose proper idioms, the right expressions and above all, a form that should be lyrical. Since caste rules did not allow Dalits to express themselves, the first generation of Dalit poets spoke whatever they wanted to speak without bothering about form and language. This led upper-caste critics to say that Dalit poems did not read like 'proper' poems. But that is not true. A case in point is the poetry of Namdeo Dhasal, a Maharashtrian and one of the finest Dalit poets. His first collection of poems, *Golpitha,* was published in 1972, the year the Dalit Panthers were formed. Using the language of the slum, Dhasal depicts many forms of caste violence in the famous red light area of Kamatipura in Bombay (now Mumbai). *Golpitha* was translated by Dilip Chitre, himself a distinguished Marathi poet, who praises the highly poetic qualities of Dhasal in the following words:

> *Golpitha* is a landmark in the history of not only Marathi but the whole of South Asian literature. In this slim book of poems we find for the first time the voice of "the scum of the earth" rising high above the sophisticated murmur of "literary" poetry without compromising its artistic authenticity and intensity. Namdeo is a big poet in the sense that Whitman, Mayakovsky, and Neruda are big. His poetry contains, unlike theirs, large chunks of a real and dirty world peopled by the have-nots and speaking their many slangs. Henry Miller once said, "I am not creating values; I defecate and nourish." Namdeo did precisely this for Marathi poetry. He restored its soil-cycle by feeding it the very excrement and garbage that could fertilize it for the future. (Bhagavan and Feldhaus 181)

Taking Marathi Dalit poetry as an example of how Dalit voices echo in Dalit writing, Ramakrishnan goes on to say how Dalit literature – be it poem, story or autobiography – has to be read very differently:

> This body of writing is not amenable to description and interpretation along purely literary, formalistic lines. The Dalit writers succeed in emphasizing the fact that the dominant view is the view of the dominant. In recent literary history no other group of writers has so unequivocally asserted the fact that literary texts are not received as single entities but within institutional frameworks. This element of self-criticism in their works is achieved by an engagement with the problem of representation of the Dalit experience in the mainstream literary traditions. The Dalit writer makes himself heard by speaking against the oppressive limitations of the prevailing traditions. (97)

Dalit poetry has begun a new literary tradition in India. Dalit poets have drawn our attention to different forms of caste and class exploitations through their poetry from the 1970s onward. After the 1990s, their poetry underwent tremendous changes in terms of focus. Ambedkar became an iconic image in almost all Dalit poetry, irrespective of language, region and nationality. Ambedkar replaced M. K. Gandhi, Bhagat Singh and even Lord Rama. Akshaya Kumar, in his book titled *Poetry, Politics and Culture* (2009), traces this trajectory in a vivid manner:

> In dalit poetry of post-1990s, Ambedkar receives singular attention and he is projected as a demi-god across regions and languages. It is interesting to observe that while in mainstream politics as well as literature, Gandhi's myth of mahatma undergoes a very uncharitable, if not hostile, dismantling; in dalit-domain, Ambedkar, after momentarily losing ground to the Panthers, not only regains ground, he stands resurrected literally as a Christ reborn. The post-Ambedkarite phase of dalit politics is more a confirmation and continuation of Ambedkarite poetics than its negation or critical rejection. (287)

Dalit poetry has undergone further changes over the years. With new themes, styles and languages it has made a distinguished place for itself in the Indian literary field. Basudev Sunani's *Cast Out* (Odia, 2008), N. D. Rajkumar's *Give Us This Day a Feast of Flesh* (Tamil, 2010) and Meena Kandasamy's *Miss Militancy* (English, 2012) are but a few examples of new Dalit poetry coming out from different languages and regions in India.

After poetry, autobiography is the most commonly used genre in Dalit literature. The very emergence of Dalit autobiographies is an act of resistance because Dalits use this as an opportunity to assert their identities through their writing. Because of a lack of access to education, it was only from 1951 onwards that Dalit autobiographies have become available in the market. Hazari's *Untouchable: An Autobiography of an Indian Outcaste* (English, 1951), Kumud Pawde's *Antasphot* (Marathi, 1981), Sharankumar Limbale's *Akkarmashi* (Marathi, 1984), Bama's *Karukku* (Tamil, 1992), Balwant Singh's *An Untouchable in the IAS* (English, 1997), Omprakash Valmiki's *Joothan* (Hindi, 1997), Baby Kamble's *Jina amucha* (Marathi, 1986; translated as *The Prison We Broke* in 2008) and Urmila Pawar's *Ayadana* (Marathi, 2003; translated as *The Weave of My Life* in 2008) are well known Dalit autobiographies, among others. Like Dalit poetry, this genre too cannot be appreciated or evaluated according to existing aesthetic and critical upper-caste literary traditions. Many of these narratives have not, in fact, been written down. They have been orally communicated and then recorded by others. For instance, the moving life-story of an unlettered ex-'untouchable' Muli, *Untouchable: An Indian Life History* (English, 1979), has been recorded by the American anthropologist James Freeman. Work like this demands a new critical orientation.

The growing number of Dalit autobiographies today is a clear instance of how Dalits have been breaking down an age-old barrier of silence. The Dalit autobiography is very distinct and different from the non-Dalit autobiography in more ways than one. For instance, at the end of every upper-caste/class autobiography there is always a sense of fulfilment. So far we do not find this in any Dalit autobiography. Instead, every Dalit autobiographer, till the very end of the narrative, is unsettled and insecure about his/her social position. The 'untouchable' self still looms large even though the person has individually achieved professional distinction – becoming a vice-chancellor, professor, doctor, lawyer, engineer or a top bureaucrat in the Indian civil service. This brings a certain tension into every narrative. The fact that every title of Dalit autobiography has a sub-title that refers to 'untouchable' life makes it clear that the search for freedom from caste is still on.

Of late, Dalit literature has also seen the emergence of fictional representations of Dalit life in the forms of short stories, novels and drama. Compared to Dalit poetry and autobiographies, fictional texts are fewer in number. Nevertheless, their presence testifies to the fact that Dalit creativity has been seriously engaged in experimenting with different literary forms so that the 'dialogical imagination' of human freedom continues. Joseph Macwan's *Angaliyat* (Gujarati: 1986, *Stepchild*: 2004), G. Kalyan Rao's *Antarani vasantam* (Telugu: 2000, *The Untouchable Spring*: 2010), P. Sivakami's *Pazhaiyana kazhithatum* (Tamil: 1989, *The Grip of Change*: 2006), Sharankumar Limbale's *Hindu* (Marathi: 2010, *Hindu: A Novel*: 2010), Akhila Naik's *Bheda* (Odia; 2010, *Bheda*: 2017) and Meena Kandasamy's *The Gypsy Goddess* (English, 2014) are examples of novels. Ajay Navaria's *Unclaimed Terrain* (translated 2013), and Gogu Shyamala's *Father may be an Elephant and Mother only a Small*

Basket, but ... (2012) are examples of anthologies of short stories, and Premanand Gajvee's *The Strength of Our Wrists* (2013) is an example of drama. Dalit fictional narratives are, in many ways, different from the kind of fiction written by upper-caste writers. Even if they are imaginary in nature, a new kind of social realism is found in every Dalit text which makes it unique. A detailed account of this will be explored in the next chapter.

DALIT LANGUAGE

We have talked about how Dalit creativity has given birth to a new Indian language. It is important to understand how and why Dalit writers and poets use the everyday language of their home, be it a slum or a village. Peppered with slang and abusive language, Dalit creativity is a real challenge to the official 'standard' language of the upper castes. The best example of the Dalit creative expression is Namdeo Dhasal's *Golpitha,* where he uses the actual language of the street spoken in Kamatipura, the famous red-light district of Mumbai. Dhasal's language was a challenge to middle-class Marathi readers who, of course, could not understand the meaning of most of the words used. Chitre comments on the kinds of languages and dialects used in the anthology,

> Pimps, petty criminals, bootleggers, opium and hashish dealers, smugglers and retailers of smuggled goods comprise the rest of the population of this and other neighbouring areas of central Bombay. The population is cosmopolitan in the sense that it is drawn from all major religious communities and language groups in India, though it would be more appropriate to call it hybrid. The language commonly spoken is a variation of "Bombay Hindi", really a cluster of various slangs which superimposes a local idiom and non-Hindi vocabulary of different origins upon a Hindi grammatical base. (92)

Namdeo Dhasal grew up in Kamatipura. Therefore, the languages and dialects he uses in *Golpitha* come naturally to him. Language reflects one's culture. Therefore, Dalit writers are not ashamed of using their everyday language in their creations. In this context Limbale's observations are important to note:

> The view of life conveyed in Dalit literature is different from the world of experience expressed hitherto. A new world, a new society and a new human being have been revealed in literature, for the first time. The reality of Dalit literature is distinct, and so is the language of this reality. It is the uncouth-impolite language of Dalits. It is the spoken language of Dalits. This language does not recognize cultivated gestures and grammar. (33)

The damning of Dalit language is based on caste bias and the fact that most of the educated population in India either do not understand it or are offended by it. But there are literary critics who take a positive stand on Dalit writers using the everyday language of the slum or the village. One such critic is Laura R. Brueck who, in *Writing Resistance: The Rhetorical Imagination of Hindi Dalit Literature*, argues that modern Dalit literature exhibits a nuanced treatment of literary language and deserves close critical attention. She explains that Dalit language

> allows for a more careful understanding of the interstices of Dalit activism, "consciousness", and literary expression. The "resistance" of these texts is thus not in the rejection of those conventions . . . rather their strategic and self-consciousness adaptation, and it is important that we pay attention to these adaptations if we are to understand the full range of innovative styles of resistance developed in Dalit writing. (8)

Brueck is right because Dalit writers deliberately use everyday language to challenge the hegemonic language of the upper castes. It is unfortunate that non-Dalit writers, instead of appreciating Dalit language, severely criticise it. Dalit writers are (naturally) insulted by this attitude and talk about this in various ways. Arun Kamble, a Marathi Dalit poet, addresses the issue in his poem 'Which Language Should I Speak?':

> Chewing trotters in the badlands
> my grandpa,
> the permanent resident of my body,
> the household of tradition heaped on his back,
> hollers at me,
> "You whore-son, talk like we do.

> Talk, I tell you!"
> Picking through the Vedas
> his top-knot well-oiled with ghee,
> my Brahmin teacher tells me,
> "You idiot, use the language correctly!"
> Now I ask you,
> Which language should I speak? (Dangle 54)

On the surface, the poem reads like a fight between a Dalit 'dialect' and brahmin 'language'. But as we go deeper there is a definite hint of the struggle around what constitutes a literary language for Dalits. By choosing to express themselves in their everyday language, Dalit writers are seeking to incorporate Dalit vocabularies into Indian literary discourse. While this should be seen as a welcome step, there is a tension over the introduction of a new language and newer vocabularies in the Indian literary scene. E. V. Ramakrishnan maps this process in the following words:

> The distance between the dialect of the caste spoken at home and the refined speech of the middle class charts the social space that divides the marginalised forms of popular speech and the imperatives of the authoritative centres of language. It is the latter which is patronised by most of the writers and the popular media. This is why the Dalit writer is forced to problematise the very concept of literary language. The literariness of language is an abstraction which serves the purpose of the dominant class by legitimating the authority invested in the "official" language. (98)

Dalit writers use Dalit language in their creative writing to resist the imposition of an official language and to also assert the legitimacy of their own vocabularies. Thus, language becomes an instance of Dalit assertion. But Dalit communities have several tongues. So their writings are linguistically diverse and different from one another. How does a Dalit text travel from one place to another?

Translation and Dalit Literature

Since Dalit writers mostly write in Indian languages, translation plays an important role in acquainting readers with otherwise inaccessible texts. Since any text conveys the language and essence of a culture, translation aims to help readers make sense of that cultural context by inscribing the new meanings onto the recipient language. Translation becomes a complex activity because the translator has to not only know the language of the text but also its associate grammar and metaphors. Rita Kothari, in her *Translating India* (2006), emphasises this point: '[i]t should also be noted that the terms "translation" and "metaphor" both share similar connotations of carrying "carrying across" or "transferring" through their etymology. Translations serve as any metaphor of understanding the "other", and metaphor itself acquires a sense of translation' (1).

When it comes to translating Dalit literature an attempt is usually made to translate a Dalit text from one regional language to English and rarely from one Indian language group to another. This is because English is considered to be a link language in many parts of India. Translating Dalit texts into English enables Dalit literature to reach a global audience. So far as translating a Dalit text from an Indian language to English is concerned, there is no one kind of English language. In fact, there are as many kinds of Indian English in India as there are Indian states. Also, in some cases English does not have the vocabulary to support the translation of certain community-specific terms and ideas which can only be transliterated, adding to the complexity of language and meaning. Translating from one Indian language to another is equally problematic. First of all, the dilemma before the translator is the selection of the text. Which text is to be chosen? Why that particular text? What is the purpose for choosing that particular text over similar texts? Also, while translating the text, the translator has to judge whether it is more important to translate the language accurately or merely convey the thought while changing the language? K. Suneetha Rani, in her article 'Does Translation Empower a Dalit Text?', cautions us in this regard:

> Keeping in mind the limitations of a language, it is more important that the idea or the thought should be conveyed "correctly". But when language is intertwined with thought, then conveying only the thought without paying attention

> to language may not be possible and it may turn out to be not empowerment of the text but a defeat of the text and its purpose. Hence the question remains, is the availability of the text alone considered empowerment of a text? Can its availability in English contribute to its empowerment? It may reach more number of readers. But the empowerment of Dalit literature has been achieved already when a Dalit writer has articulated his/her experiences and feelings which come from the deep sense of pain and shame. . . . (63)

All translators understand that no matter what language one chooses to translate from and into, the process of translation does result in a loss of meaning as many of the cultural connotations located in the original text do not get highlighted. But translation is, more importantly, an act of empowerment because it is through translation that readers are able to access, appreciate and be moved by texts in languages which would have been otherwise difficult for them to follow. This process gains much more significance in terms of Dalit writing because Dalit texts travel much more space in terms of sharing the authors' lived experiences and, in the process, mobilise opinions against caste exploitation and oppression when they are translated into English and other languages. Thus, translating Dalit texts from one language to another or into English helps both Indians and a global audience understand Indian society better. Out of the many Dalit texts that perform such functions, special reference must be made here to Omprakash Valmiki's *Joothan* (Hindi: 1997; English: 2003), Sharankumar Limbale's *Akkarmashi* (Marathi: 1984; *The Outcaste*: 2003) and Baby Kamble's *Jina amucha* (Marathi: 1986; *The Prisons We Broke*: 2009) where the idea of social justice and Dalit empowerment come together forcefully. For example, while Valmiki and Limbale, in their respective autobiographies, expose the hypocrisies of upper-caste custom and tradition, Baby Kamble delves deep into the details of the gender inequality mahar Dalit women had to live with in a patriarchal set-up. It is only through such Dalit texts that we are able to publicly debate and discuss themes such as tradition, culture, language, gender, class and religion, apart from caste.

DALIT MYTHOLOGY

One of the defining factors of any aesthetic and literary culture is its mythology – where it is sourced from, how it is interpreted and retold and the kind of social and value systems it seeks to engender. Defining 'myth', Jan Knappert, in *Indian Mythology*, writes, 'Myth is not a subject which a scientist could study, since there is no palpable evidence for it. But if a sceptic regards as "mere myth'" which a believer presents as factual truth, then that sceptic will place himself outside the world of the believer. He will never understand other peoples' (10).

Upper-caste Indian literature is full of myths depicting Dalits as the 'evil' counterparts of 'good' upper-caste people. Whether it is Vedic literature or the two Indian epics, the *Ramayana* and the *Mahabharata,* or the puranas, they are full of references to the Asuras and Rakshasas, describing them as evil, despicable and demonic. Dalit writers believe that these descriptions are an attempt at 'damning' the indigenous people of the land – the Adivasis and the Dalits. Dalit writers, therefore, strongly condemn these myths and have attempted to create new myths to counterattack these non-Dalit writings.

The most popular mythical characters Dalit writers bring into limelight are Karna, Vidura and Ekalavya from the *Mahabharata*; Sita, Ravana and Shambuka from the *Ramayana*; Buddha and Ambedkar and many others. They also use many birds and beasts such as the owl, dog and donkey as totemic representations of the various aspects of Dalit communities. The victims of the caste order become heroes and heroines in Dalit writing. Dalit writers believe that such a deconstruction of Indian upper-caste myths is necessary because mythical values have larger implications for prevalent belief systems. Baburao Bagul, a prominent Dalit writer from Maharashtra, in his article 'Dalit Literature is but Human Literature', talks about how upper-caste mythology has treated lower-caste characters such as Karna and Ekalavya:

> Heroes such as Karna and Ekalavya are, as a matter of fact, reconciled to the *varna* system; they are courageous, but because they have been denied the place they deserved in the system,

> they view life only in terms of suffering; these heroes, because they have been rejected by religion, become simply toys in the hands of fate. Such heroes offer a lot of suffering, high drama, a good deal of conflict and intense aesthetic pleasure; they easily offer an opportunity to express a fatalistic ideology, which is nothing but taking refuge in religion in order to adjust to the demands of a class-society. . . . The portrayal of such a hero offers the reader the pleasure of revisiting his own experience. Such works of art manifest nothing but Hindu mythical values and consciousness. However modernist its appearance may be, literature which conforms to such ideals is reactionary. (Dangle 285)

As Bagul seems to be saying, characters such as Karna and Ekalavya are mythologised as representatives of the lower castes and their victimisation by the caste system is sanitised by decreeing it a vagary of fate or an accident of birth. Karna was deserted by Kunti after his birth and was adopted by Adhirath, a charioteer and shudra by caste. Throughout his life Karna was insulted by the Pandavas as being 'lowborn' and was finally killed by Arjun, his natural younger brother. Ekalavya, a tribal boy, was rejected by Drona, the brahmin teacher of the Pandavas, as his disciple. Undeterred, Ekalavya made a statue of Drona and practised archery. When Drona saw his expertise, he immediately asked for his thumb as *gurudakshina*, a symbol or token of appreciation asked for by the teacher in recognition of the teaching that has taken place. Thus, Ekalavya becomes permanently handicapped and mutilated. Dalit writers have sought to retell these myths foregrounding the low-caste status and treatment of such characters. A new reading of these myths will go a long way because in India sometimes myths are read as histories and therefore, are used to maintain the status quo. Gail Omvedt, an eminent social scientist, in *Understanding Caste*, cautions us about the need for Indian myths to be re-examined from new perspectives so that the genuine voice of low castes, women, tribals and non-Aryans can be heard. She writes,

> Shambuk was not silent, he was silenced; his voice was not recorded. Ekalavya may well have fought, but his fight has been erased from myths. In many cases though, the resistance was at least partially recorded, sometimes in the written

> versions of the legends and sometimes in folk versions that had to be recovered, searched out, and brought to a position of hegemony. These may seem obvious points, something that any social scientist and historian interpreting popular mythology knows: the document itself has been produced in a social process. It should not be necessary in these days of deconstructionism and post-modernism to point this out. But it has become necessary to repeat such points because even the academic interpretations of Indian culture, the ones most influenced by supposedly sophisticated methodologies, have very often taken the high-caste versions of the myths for granted, as texts which are taken to be the unexamined basis for theorising. (102)

The academic world generally ignores myths which have existed in oral forms among Dalit communities for centuries. Most Dalit mythology and history has, by necessity, been entirely orally transmitted. Some literate Dalits, of course, have tried to document those stories in written form. *Jambavapuranam,* written in Telugu by an anonymous madiga poet, is an example of the latter. The purana is composed in the form of a conversation between a brahmin and a madiga, one of the major Dalit communities of Andhra Pradesh. The subject of conversation is how the madigas lost their caste power/status due to the machinations of the brahmins:

> Harishchandra stood for truth.
> He sold his wife and sold himself
> to serve at the funeral ground.
> Who bought him? It was our man,
> the master of the funeral ground.
> We Madigas were kings.
> Won't you agree it was so?
> Or would you argue it was all
> Viswamitra's magic? (Purushotham et al. 4)

Dalit writers are and have been rewriting Indian myths in new ways. But the problem with Dalit writing is that it is mostly written in Indian languages and hardly in English. Therefore, the 'newness' it generally advocates gets confined to a particular language because of certain issues related to translation that we have talked about in the previous section. For example, Jagannath Malik, an Odia Dalit poet, has written an alternative *Ramayana* where he interprets Rama as an Aryan king whose sole agenda is to punish the Adivasis and Dalits and uphold *varnashrama dharma*. The demons, monkeys, birds and bears mentioned in the *Ramayana*, Malik suggests, are none other than the indigenous people of the land who are unnecessarily punished because they do not subscribe to the upper-caste *varna* order. Rama's killings of Tadaka, Bali, Ravana and Shambuka are some examples of how the ruling establishment of every age desperately wants to preserve and propagate the *varna* order.

Apart from rewriting Indian myths, Dalit writers are also creating new myths to initiate debates around caste questions in present day India. Two examples of this are Cho Dharman's *Koogai* (Tamil, 2005, *The owl*) and Devanoor Mahadeva's *Kusumabale* (Kannada, 1988). In *Koogai* the owl is a revered bird worshipped by Dalit communities. During the course of the narrative, Dharman compares the position of the owl to that of Dalits in Indian caste society. The owl is never allowed by other birds to come out during the day. If at all it ventures out, the owl is attacked, teased and even pecked at by smaller birds. Like the owl, Dalits are never allowed to better themselves by the members of the caste society. If at all they try to improve their lot, they are always punished by the upper castes. Thus, the owl becomes an evocative symbol of all the oppressed communities.

Devanoor, on the other hand, invokes the supernatural to narrate the death of a young Dalit man (Channa) who falls in love with a young upper-caste woman. Channa is murdered by the upper castes as retaliation for his 'transgression'. Devanoor uses the supernatural to narrate the everyday caste realities of Dalit life and to acknowledge Dalit mythology.

CONCLUSION

The emergence of Dalit literature indicates that Dalits have now become speaking subjects. In support of the project of Dalit emancipation and freedom for those who are oppressed and exploited in the name of caste and religion, since the 1970s Dalit writers have been systematically creating a new literature with a new vocabulary. They have also been creating a new aesthetic based on the ideas of liberty, equality and human freedom. In order to make their voices heard, Dalit writers have experimented with all literary forms: poetry, autobiography, novels, short stories and drama.

Compared to Dalit poetry and autobiography, the novel began to be used by Dalit writers much later. That is because novel writing seems to be a very different kind of project where, as Mikhail Bakhtin suggests, 'dialogic imagination' is possible. Since the Dalit emancipation project needs such a dialogical imagination centering around caste, how do we read Dalit novels vis-á-vis Indian novels written by the upper castes? In other words, what are the special characteristics of a Dalit novel? How does one approach it? Which are the different methodologies that can be applied to appreciate its dynamism? These and many other questions pertaining to reading a Dalit novel will be taken up in the next chapter.

REFERENCES

Abraham, Joshil K., and Judith Misrahi-Barak, ed. *Dalit Literatures in India*. New Delhi: Routledge, 2016. Print.

Bhagavan, Manu, and Anne Feldhaus. *Claiming Power from Below: Dalits and Subaltern Question in India*. New Delhi: Oxford UP, 2011. Print.

Brueck, Laura R. *Writing Resistance: The Rhetorical Imagination of Hindi Literature*. New York: Columbia UP, 2014. Print.

Chitre, Dilip. 'The Architecture of Anger: On Namdeo Dhasal's "Golpitha".' *Journal of South Asian Literature*. Volume 17. Issue No. 1 (Winter–Spring 1982): 93–95. Print.

Dangle, Arjun, ed. *Poisoned Bread: Translations from Modern Marathi Dalit Literature*. Bombay: Orient Longman, 1994. Print.

Das, Sisir Kumar. 'The Narrative of Suffering: Caste and the Underprivileged.' *Translating Caste*. Ed. Tapan Basu. New Delhi: Katha, 2002. Print.

Gajarawala, Toral Jatin. *Untouchable Fictions: Literary Realism and the Crisis of Caste*. New York: Fordham UP, 2013. Print.

Ganguly, Debjani. *Caste and Dalit Lifeworlds: Postcolonial Perspectives*. New Delhi: Orient BlackSwan, 2008. Print.

Khandekar, Tarachand. 'Literature of Revolt and Resurgence'. *The First All India Dalit Writers Conference: A Commemorative Volume*. Ed. Bojja Tharakam. Hyderabad: Dr B. R. Ambedkar Memorial Trust, 1994. Print.

Knappert, Jan. *Indian Mythology*. London: Diamond Books, 1995. Print.

Kothari, Rita. *Translating India*. New Delhi: Cambridge UP, 2006. Print.

Kumar, Akshaya. *Poetry, Politics and Culture: Indian Texts and Contexts*. Delhi: Routledge, 2009. Print.

Kumar, Raj. *Dalit Personal Narratives: Reading Caste, Nation and Identity*. New Delhi: Orient BlackSwan. 2010. Print

Limbale, Sharankumar. *Towards an Aesthetic of Dalit Literature: History, Controversies and Cosiderations.* Trans. Alok Mukherjee. New Delhi: Orient BlackSwan, 2004. Print.

Nagaraj, D. R. *The Flaming Feet and Other Essays: The Dalit Movement in India*. Ranikhet: Permanent Black, 2010. Print.

Omvedt, Gail. *Understanding Caste: From Buddha to Ambedkar and Beyond*. New Delhi: Orient BlackSwan, 2011. Print.

Purushotham, K., et al. *The Oxford India Anthology of Telugu Dalit Writing*. New Delhi: Oxford UP, 2016. Print.

Ramakrishnan, E. V. *Making It New: Modernism in Malayalam, Marathi and Hindi Poetry*. Shimla: Indian Institute of Advanced Study, 1995. Print.

Rani, K. Suneetha. "Does Translation Empower a Dalit Text?". *Language Forum* 33.1 (2007): 55–64. Print.

Sreenivasan, S. "Why Does Dalit Literature Matter?". *Beyond Borders* 6:1–2 (2010): 24–28. Print.

Valmiki, Omprakash. *Dalit sahitya ka saundarya shastra*. New Delhi: Radhakrishna, 2001. Print.

Chapter Five

Dalit Criticism in Practice

AKHILA NAIK'S *BHEDA*

We have seen how Dalit literature enabled the articulation of the growing aspirations of Dalits in a new language and also provided new perspectives on Indian society, culture and philosophy. The previous chapter briefly explored how Dalit literature has redefined Indian aesthetics, literary language, and literary genres such as poetry and autobiography. The Dalit novel, as mentioned earlier, came to be used rather late in the Dalit literary movement but has become a very important part of how Dalit writers negotiate their 'dialogic imagination' in Indian caste society. Along with delving into the Dalit novel it also becomes important to talk about Dalit literary criticism – its tenets, formulation and practice. Unfortunately, there is very little work available on Dalit literary criticism. Most of these criticisms are written in Indian languages rather than in English. The present chapter demonstrates how Dalit literary criticism may be used to interpret a text. Dalit criticism, like Dalit literature, is comparatively new and there has been hardly any theorisation so far on the subject. I will, therefore, take the help of the existing literary and cultural theories in order to interpret a Dalit text. For this, I have chosen Akhila Naik's *Bheda* (2010), which is considered to be the first Odia Dalit novel. While dealing with *Bheda*, I will also refer to a few Dalit novels written in Indian languages so that a comparative analysis can be made.

Before we begin to analyse the idea and form of a Dalit novel and literary criticism, several questions need to be asked. What is the main discourse of the Dalit novel? How does the author negotiate various issues prevalent in caste society and society in general? What is the structure of a Dalit novel? Does it use special language? In order to begin answering these questions it would be useful to briefly look at the history of the novel in India so that we can situate the Dalit novel in its proper context.

THE EMERGENCE OF THE NOVEL IN INDIA

The origin of the novel as a literary genre in India can be traced to the coming of the British, who introduced English as a link language between the ruler and the ruled. The famous Macaulay Minute of 1835 ensured that English became the medium of instruction in educational institutes. It was in 1857, the year of the Sepoy Mutinies/ First War of Independence, that the British government established universities in Bombay, Calcutta and Madras. This paved the way for forming a set of English-educated Indians who came into contact with Western ideas and philosophy. These middle-class Indians were privileged enough to have their writing published in the newly available newspapers and journals. Bengali literature seems to have emerged before those from the rest of India as the British had been settled in that province the longest. T. W. Clark, author of *The Novel in India: Its Birth and Development,* writes, 'The newspaper provided Bengalis with a wider scope for literary activity, and soon prose narrative contributions, some of which may be described as social tales or serialized social novels, began to be published' (11).

Pyari Chand Mitra's *Alaler gharer dulal* (1858), a prose narrative, is generally considered to be the first Bengali novel. Bakim Chandra Chatterjee was influenced by the Western novel form and wrote *Rajmohan's Wife* (1864) in English. But he soon realised that his best writing was in Bengali. His second novel, *Durgeshnandini* (1865), was therefore written in Bengali. Chatterjee went on to write fourteen novels altogether.

Baba Padmanji's *Yamuna paryatan* (1857) is considered to be the first Marathi novel. It is significant that from 1860 onwards, a number of novels were written in almost all the Indian languages. For example, Nazir Ahmad's *Mirat ul Aroos* (1869) was written in Urdu, Gauri Datt's *Devrani jethani ki kahani* (1870) in Hindi,

O. Chandu Menon's *Indulekha* (1889) in Malayalam, Bhai Bir Singh's *Sundri* (1898) in Punjabi, and so on. This suggests that most Indian writers adopted the newly available Western novel form and went about legitimising it. Meenakshi Mukherjee observes,

> Fictional texts written in different Indian languages from 1860 onwards, later identified as novels, came to be evaluated largely in terms of their closeness to Western models. The canon legitimised by literary historians was constructed on the unarticulated premise that there was a universal paradigm of novel writing and, since we were introduced to it through Europe, all subsequent narrative texts of a certain length need to be judged by the standards set there. Thus in India, literary status was conferred and the appellation "novel" bestowed only on those long narratives which best adapted this European form to incorporate local material. (viii)

Mukherjee's observation though, is applicable only to those novels which were written in the nineteenth century. In the early part of the twentieth century a variety of Indian novels – social, historical, realistic, fantasy – taking on different themes and structures, emerged. At the time education was only available to the upper-caste/class men, and so we find that most novels were written by these men. Very few women, Dalits, Adivasis or other underprivileged groups took to writing because of the lack of access to education. It was only many years after Independence that education was made available to people of all constituencies, including Dalits. Thus, literate people across castes and communities started writing novels as an act of empowerment. Dalit novels need to be read in this context.

THE ARRIVAL OF THE DALIT NOVEL

Compared to other literary forms, the Dalit novel emerged rather late. Even today there are not many Dalit novels, and the few that are available are mostly written in Indian languages. Of late, some of them are available as English translations. They are Joseph Macwan's *Angaliyat* (Gujarati: 1987, *The Stepchild* in English, 2004), P. Sivakami's *Pazhaiyana kazhithalum* (Tamil: 1989, *The Grip of Change* in English, 2006), G. Kalyana Rao's *Antarani vasantam*

(Telugu: 2000, *Untouchable Spring* in English, 2010), Sharankumar Limbale's *Hindu* (Marathi: 2003, *Hindu: A Novel* in English, 2010), Bama's *Vanmam* (Tamil: 2003, *Vendetta* in English, 2008), Akhila Naik's *Bheda* (Odia: 2010, *Bheda* in English, 2017) and Meena Kandasamy's *The Gypsy Goddess* (English: 2014). Before we discuss Akhila Naik's *Bheda* in detail, let us look at a few Dalit novels so that we understand the trends and issues they address.

Joseph Macwan's *Angaliyat*

Joseph Macwan's *Angaliyat* is said to be the first Dalit novel written in any Indian language. Published in 1986, as part of a wave of Dalit writings that burst forth after Gujarat's reservation riots of 1981 and 1985, *Angaliyat* is a gripping tale of love, heroism, humiliation, revenge and death. It vividly portrays the lives of the vankars, the weaver community, of two neighbouring villages in the Charotar district of central Gujarat. In his opening note to the novel, the author writes that most of the important characters of the weaver community were 'real' and that he spent his childhood surrounded by them. So at one level, the novel reads like a memoir without an intrusive reference to the self. At another level, it is a celebration of his land, his past and his community.

The title of the novel is significant. The word 'angaliyat' generally stands for a child who follows his/her mother to a new home after her second marriage, holding her finger, *angali.* In the novel, Gokal, Meethi's son, is the stepchild. But the title is also suggestive of the fact that Dalits are considered stepchildren in India as they have never been accepted as core members of caste society. As outcastes, they keep the nation going by producing grain, building roads, carrying night soil and performing many menial and manual activities. Despite this, they feel alienated in their own motherland. In fact, Ambedkar had once told Gandhi that he had no home.

Angaliyat is a social document about the vankars of the Charotar region. It also poses political challenges to the dominant upper caste, especially, the patels, by articulating Dalit agency. This articulation has been achieved through the creation of two powerful couples, Teeha and Meethi, and Valji and Kanku. The former two could not marry each other because of caste restrictions though they loved each other. The latter enjoyed a happy but short married life. Both couples fight oppressive social structures set up by vicious patidars as well as vankar caste leaders. Macwan has also asserted the quest for Dalit identity and dignity through Teeha and Valji's resistance to caste tyranny at the cost of their lives. Meethi's vow to live with Teeha without marrying him and Kanku's decision to deny herself a physical relationship with Danji (who is now her husband but was earlier her brother-in-law) reinforces Dalit dignity. By making his characters strong, courageous, heroic and willing to sacrifice their personal impulses and desires to uphold high moral values, Macwan is scripting a new image of Dalit identity by countering the stereotypical image of Dalits as being lazy, quarrelsome, drunkards, thieves, etc., usually enforced by upper-caste writers. However, upon re-reading, this Dalit assertion of identity seems somewhat paradoxical in that the author seems to rely heavily on brahminical tropes of what constitutes a 'good' man or woman. In this novel, the Dalit men assert and legitimise their identity through physical valour, and the Dalit women assert theirs through the notion of purity and chastity.

Kalyana Rao's *Untouchable Spring*

Macwan's *Angaliyat* is really the exception rather than the rule when it comes to using upper-caste ideologies, especially the brahminical kind, to assert Dalit identity. There are other Dalit novelists who do not hesitate to prescribe violence as a means to demolish brahminical hegemony and bring about a new social order in Indian society. For example, Kalyana Rao, in *Untouchable Spring,* suggests that an armed rebellion is the only way to solve Dalit problems. This viewpoint needs to be discussed in some detail.

Untouchable Spring powerfully captures the different forms of atrocities inflicted on Dalits in erstwhile Andhra Pradesh. This is done through the reminiscences of Ruth, who recalls the story of her husband Reuben's ancestors, their own story and that of their children and grandchildren. Together it forms an epic that captures the movement and growth of six generations of a mala family. The novel is an attempt to (re)write the history of two Dalit communities, the malas and madigas, who are believed to have no history according to upper-caste Hindus. Yagati Chinna Rao, a Dalit historian, writes,

> The crucial significance of history in post-colonial societies lies not only in the "retrieval of the past but also in constructing identities." Historical enterprise in our country is thus confronted with an apparent crisis in the very selective appropriation of the past. Thus "history-less" communities pose a challenge both in terms of history writing and reconstitution of a broader social base for rebuilding the nation state. Thus, the study of such excluded groups is of immense relevance on account of the inherent radical democratic identity of their movement that offers a critique to the project of the nation state. (3)

Kalyana Rao appropriates the structure of the *Mahabharata* and the *Bhagavad Gita* by dividing his text into eighteen chapters. He also appropriates brahminical names for his Dalit characters such as Sivaiah, Venkatanarsu, Subhadra and Sasirekha, among others.

Writing about caste occupations, Rao observes how a mala or a madiga is always a bonded labourer in the village. He describes how the Karnam (the village chief who usually hails from a higher caste) very cleverly maintains a divide between the malas and the madigas. They are made to work on the Karnam's fields with their only wage being an afternoon meal. They are given three small baskets of grain per house as the 'Karnam's largesse' and fight amongst themselves for the few grains that are left on the ground. The malas and madigas are not allowed to draw water from the village well. The Dalits have to wait for some 'kind hearted' upper castes to give them some water. The book chronicles many more degrading examples of caste oppression. It talks about how brahmins would stamp out the first sign of Dalit creativity through violent means. No Dalit would be allowed to reach beyond a certain station for fear of revolt or overturning of the caste system. Dalit consciousness and expression are ruthlessly stamped out by any means possible. Rao attacks the institution of caste when he says,

> Who is the creator? Half man. Half animal. Not god. Not devil. Not man. Not monkey. A terribly distorted shape that

> no other living being had . . . That half animal is Manu. That terribly distorted Manu. He expounded the *dharmas*, special dharmas, expounded the principles of the caste system. They say he is only one. The *puranas* say that he is not one but many. They say the ones born of him are human beings. Why then could he not see Yellanna as a human being? (15)

Rao then traces how change comes to the malas and madigas once they become conscious of their basic rights to land, water and knowledge. The first sign of revolt comes from Narigadu and Mattaiah when they break tradition and forcibly occupy the village mound to save their lives from the flood. The flood makes them realise: 'We aren't born only to die . . . We are also born to kill' (35). Later in the novel, a drought forces these communities to migrate; in the end, they convert to Christianity which allows them access to education. However, they soon realise that 'though the religion has changed, the caste has not worn off' (174).

It is interesting that towards the end of the novel, Rao suggests that one of the possible solutions to the problems of the Dalit community is to join an armed struggle. Though Immanuel, Ruth and Reuben's only son, is killed in a fake encounter with the police, Ruth and Reuben are proud of Immanuel because he sacrifices his life for the liberation of his people. Knowing the risks involved, Ruth and Reuben encourage their grandson Jesse and his wife Ruby to commit their lives to the fight for justice and liberation of their people.

Rao also must be praised for using new techniques to narrate Dalit lives in his novel. Apart from giving the novel the structure of an epic, Rao narrates the stories through the voice of Ruth, a Dalit woman. The histories and stories of these communities are therefore seen through the usually unheard perspective of a lower-caste female. However, how far is Rao able to give agency to Dalit women, is a question that needs to be considered and is often asked by Dalit women writers themselves.

Sivakami's *The Grip of Change*

In *The Grip of Change,* Sivakami portrays Kathamuthu, a Dalit patriarch and politician, who sexually exploits women of all castes, both Dalit and non-Dalit. Through Gowri, Kathamuthu's daughter and a college-educated Dalit woman, Sivakami offers a gendered critique of Dalit leadership. Sivakami seems to suggest that, since the Dalit movement is all about equality and dignity for Dalits, the Dalit leadership must consider the gender question while fighting against caste. Otherwise, the Dalit movement cannot be inclusive. This narrative strategy employed by a Dalit woman novelist must be praised because such a nuanced and open criticism of one's own community is rare in the history of Indian literature. Meena Kandasamy, while reviewing the novel, writes,

> In *The Grip of Change*, a novel of critical realism, Gowri views her father Kathamuthu, the local Dalit leader, with an attitude of contempt. By speaking of his tyrannical overbearingness, corruption and polygamy, Sivakami has reflected the universal trend that powerful men usually lead pathetic lives. Here, the acute portrayal of Kathamuthu and the women in his life, captures the unseen, unedited side of Dalit patriarchy. The significance of the book lies in the fact that it speaks for the most vulnerable members of the Dalit community – its women. (Sivakami 193–94)

Sivakami is not the only Dalit woman writer who is critical about Dalit patriarchy. Bama in her two-part autobiography in Tamil, *Karukku* (1992) and *Sangati* (1994), and Baby Kamble in her famous autobiography *The Prisons We Broke* (Marathi, 1986) have extensively dealt with the issue of Dalit patriarchy. Such a nuanced view of Dalit communities is necessary for the Dalit movement to truly become an inclusive movement.

CONTEXTUALISING AKHILA NAIK'S *BHEDA*

Compared to *Angaliyat*, *Untouchable Spring* and *The Grip of Change*, Akhila Naik's *Bheda* is different in many ways because Naik, following Ambedkar's ideology, tries to bring about a balance between all the different constituencies these authors have talked about in their respective novels. Apart from caste questions, *Bheda* addresses issues related to education, environment, gender, local history, the media, police and Hindu fundamentalism. Coming more than one hundred and twenty years after Umesh Chandra Sarkar's *Padmamali* (1888), which is considered to be the first Odia novel, this novel, for the first time, addresses caste questions in Odisha in a major way. Odia society has witnessed several social protest movements against caste at different periods in time. *Bheda* takes those debates further. As mentioned in the previous chapter, criticism of Dalit literature cannot be undertaken without an understanding of the contexts out of which the particular text has arisen. To that end, we will briefly examine how caste operates in Odia civil society to better understand the questions and issues raised in the novel.

Caste and Existence in Odisha

Dalits in Odisha, as elsewhere in India, have been victims of caste oppression for centuries. Living predominantly in rural locations and illiterate, they have become one of society's most exploited peripheral groups. Over the years, they have been subjected to sub-human conditions and have suffered economic exploitation, cultural subjugation and political powerlessness. Even seventy years after Independence, many civic and other amenities are not available to them; this is because Odisha continues to be a feudal state where modern and democratic agencies have not been able to alter the traditional power structure.

Living in a hostile environment where caste determines everything, Odia Dalits have always had to work hard and lead a life of compromise, alienation and resignation. According to the 2011 Census, Odisha has 75 Dalit communities, constituting eighteen per cent of the state's population. Following the Hindu caste structure, Dalit communities too have rigid internal hierarchies among themselves. As a result, inter-caste dining and inter-caste marriages are still not allowed across Dalit communities. Dalit politics in the state is fragmented as Dalits are divided into many groups and sub-groups. They also follow different religious practices. Because of these problems Dalits cannot come together to voice their grievances. Dalit groups are split and fragmented, each carrying the tag of being a Dalit.

The brahmins, karanas, khandayats and other upper-caste communities still wield what might be called 'historical power' and continue to exploit and oppress Dalits. Though they can move freely in towns and cities, there are several restrictions on them in villages where they are still confined to the outskirts. For example, they cannot walk on certain roads nor may they ride a cycle because they are said to be carriers of 'pollution'. They are not allowed to enter temple premises. Even though they can go to school, their children are not allowed to sit with the upper-caste children. They have separate wells and in the ponds, there are separate *ghats* where they may bathe. They have separate burial grounds as well. To this day such discrimination is practised, strengthening the walls and barriers of social difference.

Though education might significantly improve their lives, both socially as well as economically, Dalits have never been able to get its benefits on a large scale due to typical structural problems in Odisha. For example, almost all the government education institutions in the state are headed by upper-caste people who generally discriminate against Dalits. The persistent caste practices in schools, colleges and universities are so common that Dalit children have no other option but to discontinue their studies.

As a result, the level of literacy among Dalits in Odisha is quite low even today. Apart from not getting any secure jobs, Dalits in Odisha cannot avail of many of the constitutional provisions that guarantee them a life of dignity and self-respect. Struggling to meet their daily needs Odia Dalits, therefore, cannot think of organising a movement against their oppressors. That no militant movement or rebellion on the part of Dalits has taken place against their upper-caste Hindu counterparts in the state only underlines the fact that Odia Dalits have endured caste oppression silently, not that the oppression and inequalities do not exist. One reason for this could be that the socio-economic life of Dalits in Odisha has not undergone the same level of change as that of Dalits elsewhere, for example, in Maharashtra. History suggests that a few cases of unorganised, sporadic resistance did take place but were swiftly suppressed. It also seems to be that whenever there was any protest against caste oppression, the upper-castes always succeeded in appropriating the dissenting voices. As a result, the voices of the oppressed gradually fade away. This is something we see when we traverse the pages of Odisha's socio-cultural and literary history.

Social Protest Movements in Medieval Odisha

Violent eruptions of frustration and anger by Dalits against caste oppression have been rare; however, since the fifteenth century, many voices, particularly through literary forms, have been raised against inequality and injustice. Sudramuni Sarala Dasa in the fifteenth century was a pioneer of the medieval social protest movement in Odisha. Sarala Dasa is known for three major works, namely the *Odia Mahabharata*, the *Bilanka Ramayana*, and the *Chandi purana*. These were written in the language of the common people and dealt with topical and mundane events. He was protesting against the courtly poets and writers (who wrote in Sanskrit), against the language of dominance and power, and against royal characters and elitist themes. Sarala Dasa was a sudra by caste. At a time when Hindu orthodoxy was at its peak, we find that Sarala Dasa managed to articulate the voice of the marginalised and critique the Hindu social order. This was no mean achievement for a sudra.

Sarala Dasa's protest was carried on by five saint–poets who dominated Odia literature for a century (1450–1550). These poets were Balarama Dasa, Jagannatha Dasa, Achyutananda Dasa, Jasobanta Dasa and Ananta Dasa, collectively known as Panchasakhas. Except for Jagannatha Dasa, who was a brahmin, the rest of them were sudras. They rejected the dominance of Sanskrit in literature and espoused the cause of the vernacular as the medium of expression, thus contributing towards the use of everyday Odia in the literature of their region. In fact, they followed the path Sarala Dasa had forged and rendered sacred Hindu texts into the people's language in order to make them accessible to the people. Balaram Dasa's *Jagmohan Ramayan* and *Lakshmi puran*, Jagannatha Dasa's *Odia bhagabata*, Achyutananda Dasa's *Harivamsa*, Jasobanta Dasa's *Premabhakti brahmagita* and Ananta Dasa's *Hetudaya bhagabata* are the foremost examples of this development.

The poets also protested against the rigidities of life in temples and monasteries and sought to rise above the prejudices and debates that had reduced religion to the level of an intellectual polemic. In the process, they had to face opposition, criticism and even conspiracy from the orthodox pundits who instigated the kings against them. In spite of various repressive measures taken by the establishment, the movement could not be curbed fully, even if it had to eventually compromise with the dominant brahminical system.

After the Panchasakhas, the tradition of writing protest literature focusing on and depicting people's lives and language came to an abrupt end. A drastic change in the approach of literature both in theme as well as in style is clearly discernible. The lead was taken by the princes such as Dhananjaya Bhanja and Upendra Bhanja in the eighteenth century, who were acquainted with the themes and preoccupations of old Sanskrit works, their forms and their ornate style and articulations. Their literary works were bound to be aristocratic and there was no hint of reform or revolution in their writing.

Bhima Bhoi and his Protest against the Hindu social order

Protest literature was once again retrieved from the religious realm by Bhima Bhoi (1855–94). Born into a kondh (Adivasi) family, Bhoi was a follower of the Mahima Dharma, an autochthonous religious movement which made its presence felt in Odisha in the nineteenth century. Most of its followers were from the oppressed classes of society – the Dalits and the Adivasis. Bhima Bhoi was also a poet of distinction who composed several poems and also wrote philosophical treatises. His best known works are the *Stuti chintamani*, the *Srutinisedha gita* and the *Nirbeda sadhana*. Apart from these, there are scores of his 'Mahima' bhajans whose language is so simple that anyone can memorise them. Like his predecessors, Bhoi attacked the orthodox rituals and customs of Odia society. His literary works sought to redefine and redesign societal norms, manners and behaviour, promising the poor a better world.

Inspired by Bhima Bhoi, some of the followers of Mahima Dharma organised a protest march in 1874 to burn the idols of the Puri Jagannath temple, claiming that Lord Jagannath did not belong to the higher castes but to the original inhabitants of the state, the Adivasis and Dalits. The contention is that Jagannath was originally an Adivasi god belonging to the savara tribe. With the connivance of the Raja-brahmin nexus, over time the tribal god was Hinduised and brahmanised so much that Adivasis and Dalits were, to this day, not allowed to enter the temple. Thus Bhoi's religio-literary consciousness gave birth to an incipient organisation and movement that ventured into the newly emerging public sphere.

Of course, Bhoi's ideas and activities represented a consciousness that targeted those elements in Hindu society which did not hesitate to oppress and suppress its own members. However his message did not find expression in multiple ways and movements due to the existential situation of Dalits in Odisha. Before, and even under colonial rule, Dalits in Odisha could not take advantage of the benefits of elementary education. The British came to Odisha as late as 1803, and many modern facilities like roads, railways, telephones and telegraphs were introduced only towards the beginning of the twentieth century. Being one of the most feudal states in India, Odisha did not go through the structural changes that would otherwise have extended several opportunities to the most oppressed groups. It was only after Independence that a sizeable number of Dalits made an entry into civil society through literacy and education. However, plans for their education, though announced as government policy, could not spread effectively because of structural inequalities, economic imbalances and political chicanery. Unlike other places, pre-independence missionary support for Dalit education came late to Odisha.

The Progressives and Nationalism in Odisha

Because of the lack of education and exposure, Ambedkar and other Dalit movements during that time did not really have a literary impact among the Odia Dalits. However, during the same period we find some writings on Dalits by upper-caste writers mainly within the overarching ideology of nationalism. Kalindi Charan Panigrahi, Godabarish Mahapatra, Radha Mohan Gadanayak, Bhagabati Charana Panigrahi, Sachi Routray, Gopinath Mohanty, Kanhu Charan Mohanty, Basant Kumar Satpathy and Parshuram Mund are some of the upper-caste writers who represented lower-caste characters in their writings. Whether such a representation of Dalits amounts to 'Dalit' literature is a question that needs to be explored, but amongst Dalits there is a strong resistance to 'borrowed' experience being passed off as direct experience. However, there are at least two fascinating tales about Dalits and caste oppression told from the upper-caste perspective. One is Gopinath Mohanty's novel *Harijan* (1948) and another is Basant Satpathy's short story *Unnati* (Development, 1972). While Mohanty's work shows his pity and sympathy towards his Dalit characters, Satpathy is more nuanced about depicting Dalit subjectivity. These works, and others like them, open up the field as to who qualifies as a 'caste ally' in Dalit movements.

It was only after Independance that some educated Dalits in Odisha raised their voices in protest. Govind Chandra Seth, Santanu Kumar Das, Jagannath Malik, Kanhu Malik and Kanduri Malik came together to set up the Dalit Jati Sangha (Dalit League) in 1953. Ambedkar, who was alive then, was a great source of inspiration for this Sangha which tried to bring Dalit communities together to fight caste-related exploitations. Since many of these leaders were also creative writers they tried to raise awareness among Dalits through literarature. For example, Govind Chandra Seth wrote a biography of Ambedkar that instantly became famous. Santanu Kumar Das seems to have written four novels on caste inequalities and social injustices. The titles of the novels were *Aawhana* (A call), *Vitamati* (Homestead), *Sania* and *Pheria* (Comeback). None of these novels are traceable now. Many other Dalit leaders also started writing literature dealing with caste issues. However, their writings were markedly different from Dalit writings that came after the 1970s. The Dalit as a political subject and the radicalisation of Dalit subjectivity were missing, particularly in the Dalit writings in Odisha which came out immediately after Independence.

The Radicalisation of Odia Dalit Subjectivity

It was only in the 1970s and 80s that Odia Dalits began asserting themselves, if not organisationally, at least individually through their writings which can be said to constitute 'Dalit' literature. This is seen as the third phase of protest, which took its inspiration from the modern world view that emphasised the importance of freedom and equality. Writers of this new literature are few; most of them are teachers, lawyers, doctors and government employees and constitute a small vanguard symbolising the advanced consciousness of a very backward and divided people. However, a look at the whole spectrum of Odia Dalit writers reveals a vision that goes beyond their geographical boundary and is relevant in any part of the world.

Bichitrananda Nayak can be called a pioneer in Odia Dalit writings. In 1972, when the Dalit Panthers launched the Dalit literary movement in Maharashtra, Nayak published a collection of poems titled *Anirbana* (Liberation, 1972) using the term 'Dalit' in several places. Like Nayak, poets and writers like Jagannath Malik, Krushna Charan Behera, Govind Chandra Seth and Ramachandra Sethi exposed the hypocrisies of upper-caste Odia society. Malik is well known for his novel *Kshudhita Kharavela* (*The hungry Kharavela*, 1994) where he takes a dig at the historical character of Kharavela (a medieval Odia king) to interpret contemporary issues. Without naming anyone, through Kharavela, the writer scrutinises a modern politician – probably a chief minister of Odisha – who is both corrupt as well as autocratic. Malik's second important work is a version of the *Ramayana* where he reinterprets the episodic events of the epic from a Dalit point of view. He imagines Rama as an Aryan king who goes to the jungle in order to teach the Adivasis and Dalits a lesson or two.

Krushna Charan Behera, Gobind Chandra Seth, and Ramachandra Sethi wrote on the themes of untouchability, caste exploitation, gender inequality and class oppression, and tried to bring Dalit discourse into the arena of Odia literature in a limited way. However, it was the Ambedkar centenary celebration of 1991 that motivated a number of Odia Dalit poets and writers to write their own histories. Ambedkar's writings and speeches were made available in Odia. As a result, many educated Odia Dalits were able to read about caste-related issues and openly wrote about various facets of caste, class and gender exploitations in Odia society: Basudev Sunani, Samir Ranjan, Sanjay Bag, Gopinath Bag, Dolamani Kandher, Pitambar Tarai, Ramesh Malik, Chandrakant

Malik, Kumaramani Tanti, Supriya Malik, Basant Malik, Akhila Naik, Anjubala Jena, Mohan Jena, Samuel Dani, Anand Mahanand, Panchanan Dalei, and Pravakar Palka.

Poverty, powerlessness, untouchability, hypocrisy and corrupt social practices have generated a variety of responses from Odia Dalit writers. These responses are forms of protest aimed at bringing about change through a social revolution. Their protest is not against any individual or group but against society as a whole. They reject the so-called 'tradition' which helps upper castes legitimise existing structures of inequality. Thus, Odia Dalit literature, in all its forms, interrogates the world-view and institutions of upper castes and demands a new social philosophy and practice. Akhila Naik's *Bheda* has to be read against this background.

ATTEMPTING A DALIT CRITICAL ANALYSIS OF *BHEDA*

The Title of the Novel

Akhila Naik's *Bheda* has the distinction of being the first Odia Dalit novel after a long spell of silence. None of the previous novels by Dalits is currently available. It is a very short novel – 88 pages comprising seven chapters, each named after a character. In every chapter the novelist very deftly addresses caste questions. Before critically analysing the novel, we need to understand the etymological meaning of the title of the novel, 'bheda'.

The word 'bheda' has multiple meanings. The primary meaning is 'a sense of difference'. If 'bheda' is used with the word 'bhaba' it implies the differences that exist among people in terms of caste class or race. 'In the Indian context "bhedabhaba" (*bhed-bhav* in Hindi) basically denotes various kinds of caste discriminations the upper castes practise against the lower castes, especially Dalits.' (Kumar, 'Translator's Note' xxvii). 'Bheda' also means 'target'. In the novel, Dalits are targeted by the upper castes because, after availing themselves of modern education, Dalits are now mobilising to protest against the monopolies of the upper castes. 'Bheda' also has another meaning: 'to properly understand the "intricacies" of an incident or event' (xxviii). Thus, all the different meanings of the word are in some way or the other connected to the idea of caste and its corollary, caste discrimination and caste atrocities. By giving this powerful and multi-layered title to his novel, Naik wants to draw our attention to how complex the caste situation is in Indian society. He openly condemns the caste system; and by writing this novel, he is able to initiate a dialogue on the question of human rights and social justice in a backward state like Odisha, where such issues are rarely raised in the public domain.

Narrative Strategies

Naik's novel is a departure from the many non-Dalit novels available in the Odia language. It seems as if Naik is experimenting with form, content, language and grammar – all at the same time – in the novel. Even though it is a short novel, Naik's narrative strategies enable him to deal with caste questions in all their complexities. Because of the simple narrative structure, the novel flows freely and the author strategically uses a folk style to narrate his story. His characters debate many social issues before coming to certain conclusions. He narrates incidents in such a lively way that the readers feel as if they are witnessing, firsthand, events unfolding before them. He allows his characters to speak for themselves. Not surprisingly, his language is free from the over-Sanskritised, standard Odia register. He uses the common people's language to narrate the events. As a result many of the idioms and phrases used by the villagers of the Kalahandi region find their way into the text and enrich it. The novel expounds a new aesthetic.

The seven chapters are named after characters of the novel: Dinamastre, the school headmaster; Baya or the Mad Lawyer; Laltu, a young Dalit activist; Semi Seth, the businessman; Muna, a school drop-out Dalit who runs a tailoring shop; Mastrani, wife of the headmaster; and Santosh Panda, the correspondent of a local newspaper. These are but a few representative characters from 'small India', and yet, they are an active component of a dynamic modern Indian state, participating in the process of nation-building. Some of them sacrifice everything for this cause, whereas, others try to grab a large slice of the 'national cake'. Naik presents this national drama quite successfully; it ends in tragedy, with Dalits suffering at the hands of upper-caste hooligans.

The action of the novel largely takes place in some remote villages of the Kalahandi district in western Odisha. Towards the end of the novel the action shifts from the villages to the district headquarters of Kalahandi – Bhawanipatna – which is the centre of power and authority. Naik draws attention to this link between the village and the town, perhaps to make a point: where should Dalits live? This reminds us of Ambedkar's call to Dalits to leave the villages and go to the cities, because Indian villages, beset by caste practices, are hellish. In cities, Dalits will at least live in anonymity. Ambedkar's call is in stark contrast to Gandhi's idea of 'gram swaraj', where he finds peace and harmony among the villagers irrespective of their caste or class affiliations. In the novel, Dalits in rural India have hardly any freedom and security. Without material means and opportunity they continue to stay on, although choosing to organise protests against the monopolies of the upper castes in their villages. The result is that they face severe atrocities. Their houses and shops are burnt down by upper-caste mobs leaving them without help or hope. They are rendered homeless in their homeland. Their leader, Laltu, is implicated in a false case by the upper castes and is arrested. What are Dalits to do? Where can they go? What stake do they have in the Republic of India? Perhaps the novelist intends to ask these and many more such questions while narrating his stories of gruesome caste violence.

The Development Discourse

The novel was published in 2010 when India celebrated sixty years of being a republic. Six decades of welfare policies with equity and justice enshrined in the Indian Constitution should have been enough to eliminate poverty, illiteracy, malnutrition and all sorts of ills from India. But that did not happen. The novel takes us to Kalahandi, one of the poorest districts of India to narrate its encounter with the development discourse.

Kalahandi came into the limelight in the 1980s when national dailies carried reports of starvation deaths and the sale of children. The news attracted the attention of then Prime Minister of India, Rajiv Gandhi, who rushed to Kalahandi. Since then Kalahandi has become notorious for poverty, drought, famine, child-trafficking, mass migrations and malnutrition. The district has often been described as the 'Somalia of India' by the media. However, the ground reality is altogether different. After intense research, several social scientists have informed us that the poverty we see in Kalahandi is more manmade than a consequence of natural phenomena such as droughts, floods, etc.

In the past, Kalahandi was rich in natural resources and sixty per cent of its area was covered by dense forest. The 1950s and 60s saw India go through a series of changes under the leadership of Jawaharlal Nehru. The welfare policies which Nehru propounded and propagated during his premiership were supposed to usher in 'development' in all spheres. But that did not happen in Kalahandi. Instead, in the name of development, the Kalahandi region was uninhibitedly and openly exploited. The people of Kalahandi witnessed hundreds and thousands of trucks plying day and night on its rough roads. People still describe the scene with awe about how these trucks carried away all the valuable wood – including teak – from their deep, green jungles. This well-organised looting was conducted by builders, contractors, bureaucrats and politicians. Kalahandi, they thought, was a 'goldmine' and they extracted as much wealth as they could amass for themselves. They stripped Kalahandi of its greenery and left it barren and useless.

Apart from frequent droughts and famines, Kalahandi has massive structural inequalities that directly affect the Dalits and Adivasis, who together constitute about fifty per cent of the population in the region. The upper castes, particularly brahmins, and other subsidiary castes in the district own a major portion of the available land. They are also the ones who have availed of education and grabbed power and positions in government offices. Dalits and Adivasis, on the other hand, are mostly landless, poor and illiterate. Therefore, they are almost entirely dependent on the mercy of the upper castes for their everyday existence.

Being a resident of Kalahandi, Naik is thus an insider who has witnessed the 'development' narratives of the region. Therefore his fictional accounts can be interpreted as an attempt to rewrite the social history of Kalahandi with a special focus on Dalits.

Education as Emancipation

Naik begins his novel by underlining the significance of education in Dalit lives. His character Dinamastre is a Dalit primary school teacher. For a Dalit to become a school teacher in Kalahandi is a great achievement because such an opportunity comes but rarely to the members of marginalised communities. Dalits in Kalahandi seem to have occupied several government posts thanks to modern education and the implementation of the reservation policy. But if we look at the ground reality it seems impossible for Dalits to get jobs in places where the upper castes have occupied positions for several years. Gauging the way the upper castes have maintained their caste networks over these years, it would appear impossible for a poor Dalit like Dinabandhu Duria (Dinamastre's full name) to get a job. But modern education has made a difference. Several social changes have made it possible for Dalits to find a place in upper-caste bastions and upset the traditional power structure. It is for this reason that there is tension throughout the narrative of the novel.

Naik is very blunt in revealing the discourse of power in the novel. He provides several instances of how the upper castes feel threatened whenever a Dalit occupies any kind of formal position. Naik traces this symptom to their 'caste mindedness' which makes the upper castes think that every public institution in India is their private property. Dinamastre's new job brings him opportunities as well as challenges. His job gives him the kind of economic security which his father and forefathers could never dream of. As a teacher he also earns respect in society unlike other members of his community. He is a dedicated teacher and, after several years of struggle and hard work in public life, is now the headmaster of the primary school of his village, Firozpur. He is a simple, honest, gentle person.

It is through Dinamastre that Naik begins his caste discourse in the novel. As a Dalit writer and someone who has benefitted from modern education like Dinamastre, Naik (himself a teacher in the Government College at Bhawanipatna in Kalahandi) believes that ultimately education will free Dalits from the bondage of caste slavery. This is a significant political stand because education has remained the main agenda of Dalit movements and has been advocated by Phule and Ambedkar as well as by present day Dalit activists. Naik, while applauding the role of modern education in the Dalit emancipation project, also notices several issues responsible for overturning such a noble project.

Because of his Dalit background (he belongs to the dom community), Dinamastre is often mercilessly humiliated by his upper-caste counterparts. In the first chapter Naik describes how the school inspector, a highly educated brahmin, deliberately uses his caste name when he addresses him in the presence of his students, just to insult him. Occasionally the other upper castes do the same. Dinamastre, on his part, suffers through such caste prejudices for the sake of his family. Fearing backlash he never retaliates. His foremost aim in life is to raise his only son, Laltu, in a peaceful environment and to give him the best education possible. Contrary to his dreams, Laltu abandons his education and becomes a full-time social activist. He mobilises the Dalits and lower castes in the region to resist the monopoly of the upper castes, and becomes a celebrated leader of the cause. At the end of the novel, Laltu is falsely implicated in a case by the upper castes and goes to jail.

By creating a marked contrast between the father and the son, Naik shines a light on the radical side of Dalit politics. He critically evaluates the role of education in employment and social revolution. While the first is limited to the individual or at best to the immediate family, the second extends to the community or society. Naik thus defines the role of education not in any abstract terms but in terms of the actual role it plays in society. Therefore, we see that when Laltu grows up he becomes conscious of the plight of his community, who are treated like animals by caste society. This realisation makes him a rebel.

As a leader he is not militant but works hard to change the mindset of his people. To effect social revolution, he organises the young people of his area. His sangha guards the interests of the common people. Apart from fighting the monopoly of the upper castes, they also fight corrupt officials, local contractors, politicians and businessmen. Their activism brings a few visible changes to the region. For example, they guard the local forest when they realise that the local businessman, Semi Seth, is exporting truckloads of wood illegally. It is only when they seize his tractor and report it to the higher authorities of the forest department that Seth's looting comes to an end. Unfortunately, their activism comes to an abrupt end when the upper-caste leaders unite to take revenge on them. Dalits are beaten up by the upper castes, Dalit *bastis* (settlements) are burnt down, and they are forced to desert their homes to save their lives while the police force passively stands by, having been bribed by the upper castes. Semi Seth, the Marwari, and Banabihari Tripathy, the Mad Lawyer, both take the lead in organising this carnage.

The Insider–Outsider Dynamic

Naik brings alive the insider–outsider dynamic through Laltu, on the one hand, and Semi Seth and Banabihari Tripathy on the other. While Laltu is an insider – an 'original' inhabitant of the land – both Seth and Tripathy are 'outsiders'. Naik collects information from local history and folklore to establish the 'foreign' origins of these two. Semi Seth's father, Pawan Agrawal, is a marwari who had come empty-handed to Kalahandi from Rajasthan. He opened a small ration shop in the village of Beheda and amasses wealth illegally in no time at all. After his father's death, Semi Seth inherits his property and works through dubious means to further extend his empire. Among his possessions are a rice mill and a fleet of tractors which ply day and night to take away the best wood from the pristine jungles of Kalahandi. Semi Seth also buys food grains and forest products cheaply from the villagers and sells them at a much higher price. Even during droughts and famines his godown is never empty. Semi Seth is a representative of the marwari business community whose presence in Odisha is widespread. When locals borrowed money from the marwaris they do so knowing that they will have to pay a high rate of interest. In the 1980s, the young people of Kalahandi organised movements to evict marwaris from the region. Several riots took place in different towns and villages. But eventually the marwaris stayed on after a peace treaty was signed between the two groups in 1984.

Banabihari Tripathy's ancestors come from Uttar Pradesh. In pre-colonial times Odisha had no brahmin population and

Kalahandi was dominated by Adivasi, Dalit and Backward Caste populations. Almost all the village chiefs or *gauntias* were either Adivasis or Backward Caste people. Indeed the king of Kalahandi was an Adivasi (Deo). With the 'Hinduisation' of the Kalahandi region, it seems that Banabihari's grandfather became a temple priest. He tries to educate his son, Sachikant Tripathy, who later becomes a forester in Junagarh, Kalahandi. Sachikant makes friends with Lochan Hati, the *gauntia* of Firozpur village who belongs to a Backward Community (OBC in today's context) called gouda (who are essentially cowherds and farmers). Later Sachikant uses a trick to become the *gauntia* himself by replacing Hati. Banabihari, Sachikant's son, goes off to Calcutta (Kolkata) to study law and becomes a lawyer.

Semi Seth and Banabihari Tripathy join hands to further their interests. With the Hindutva movement spreading all over India in the 1980s and 90s, the two become self-styled protectors of Hinduism. They organise Rashtriya Swayamsevak Sangh (RSS) *shakhas* in the villages and join in the hate campaign against Muslims and Christians. Opposed to any kind of conversion, they mobilise Dalits, Adivasis and Backward Castes into joining their campaign. When Laltu starts his activism, they find him a tough opponent and initially try to harass him. But when Laltu gains the support of the people and is able to successfully resist them, they plan to teach him a lesson. They not only falsely implicate him and send him to jail but also organise mobs to perpetuate violence against the Dalits.

The insider–outsider dynamic is also demonstrated in the way Santosh Panda, a brahmin correspondent for the local newspaper, turns on Laltu in order to make sure he stays an outsider. Laltu starts writing articles on the different problems in his region in order to bring them to the notice of a larger public. In appreciation of his whole-hearted devotion to the cause of the people, Santosh Panda, correspondent for the *Hastakshep* (Intervention), recruits him as a local reporter. Panda assumes the role of a patron and supports Laltu's activism. But when a case is filed against Laltu that he incited Dalits to throw the bone of a cow into the temple, Panda begins to doubt Laltu's integrity. Laltu tries his best to prove his innocence but Panda is not convinced. He remembers that Laltu had argued during their discussions that the upper castes, including brahmins, ate beef during Vedic times and after. Though the correspondent promises to help Laltu, he succumbs to the pressure of his caste prejudice. Panda not only supports his upper-caste brethren in the fight against Dalits but also sees to it that Laltu's arrest is front-page news in order to publicise his 'misdeeds'.

Panda's diabolic role in destroying the Dalit movement is not surprising since the media is not always unbiased. This leads Naik to comment that everyone is against Dalits: civil society, state, police and the media. Social scientists seem to support Naik's argument. For example, Vidya Devi, who has researched caste-based discriminations, writes: 'Hindus control the government, the police, the judiciary, press and all else, including the military. Whenever there is any violence against Untouchables, the whole world comes down on them' (125).

Gender and Religion

Naik raises the gender issue in *Bheda* through Mastrani, Dinamastre's wife and Laltu's mother. As a Dalit woman she represents her class in the novel. But compared to many poor Dalit women of her neighbourhood who work hard for their survival, Mastrani does not have to work for a living. Being financially secure, she commands both power and social position, for which the other members of the community respect her.

Naik points out how Dalit patriarchy works to the advantage of Dalit men. Even though Mastrani is literate she sacrifices her career by prioritising her family. She shares Dinamastre's dream of seeing Laltu in a respected position. Laltu's inability to complete his education and his failure to get a good job makes Mastrani very unhappy. But throughout his activism she supports him whole-heartedly. When he comes home late at night he finds her waiting for him. If he is unable to come back home she stays up all night worrying. Thus when Laltu sacrifices his career for his community and society, it is Mastrani who sustains his dream by sacrificing her time and energy just to see a new society without caste discriminations emerge.

It is through Mastrani that the author throws light on the religious life of the Dalit community in Kalahandi district of Odisha. Dalit communities across the Kalahandi district have been traditional worshippers of Budharaja, Dokribudhi, Thutimaili, Kalisundri, etc., (non-Hindu local deities originally worshipped by Dalits, Adivasis and the lower castes of Kalahandi in the past; now, irrespective of caste, worshipped by the entire village as village deities along with other Hindu gods and goddesses like Lakshmi, Durga, Saraswati, Ganesh, Shiva, Rama and Krishna, etc.) since time immemorial. But with the Hinduisation and brahminisation of the area, Kalahandi has been flooded with Hindu gods and goddesses. Local people are often seen worshipping these new gods and goddesses, ignoring their folk deities.

As women are usually the custodians of culture, it is through the character of Mastrani that we get a glimpse into the Hinduisation of Dalit culture in the novel. After availing of modern education, getting a government job and the consequent economic security, Dinamastre's family starts worshipping Hindu deities – Mahadev in particular – which the illiterate villagers do not like. There is a debate in the novel between Majhibaba, an Adivasi who is also the village priest, and Dinamastre as to which gods and goddesses the villagers should worship. While Majhibaba argues for sticking to tradition by worshipping only folk deities, Dinamastre offers justifications as to why Hindu gods and goddesses should be worshipped along with folk deities. Even though she takes pride in Dalit culture, Mastrani imitates upper-caste lifestyles. A charitable woman, she gives alms to beggars and mendicants and helps the poor and the destitute. She bathes early in the morning, worships Hindu deities, regularly fasts and visits temples much to the satisfaction of the upper castes. Mastrani perhaps thinks that she will be accepted as one among the upper castes if she imitates their lifestyle, but she is mistaken, as she later discovers.

Unlike Mastrani, Laltu is an agnostic. He criticises his mother when she drags him to a temple. He challenges the existence of God when Mastrani tries to convince him of the significance of visiting the temple. He cites many instances from the puranas, shastras and everyday life to tell her how Hinduism as a religion discriminates against Dalits. She finally realises this when she visits the Mahadeva temple in her neighbouring village. She cannot offer worship to the deity like others from the upper castes do. She can offer her *puja* only through the brahmin temple priest. Disturbed by this she questions herself: is a Dalit not a human being? Though she realises that the caste system is a discriminatory practice of the upper-caste Hindus against Dalits, Mastrani neither points an accusatory finger at upper-caste Hindus nor attempts to correct their behaviour. She is not an activist like her son. Naik portrays Mastrani, not as a revolutionary Dalit woman, but a devoted wife and a loving mother who places her family above anything else.

CONCLUSION

Bheda exposes the double standards of Indian caste society by highlighting different forms of atrocities perpetrated on Dalits by the upper castes. Naik suggests that the idea of caste is enmeshed with violence, and violence in any form has to be condemned unequivocally by every member of civil society. He exposes the roles of various agencies of the Indian nation-state – including the police, the administration, the education system and the media – as being hand in glove with the upper castes and part of the problem. Apart from the caste question, Naik also raises important issues such as the idea of conversion, the role of the media and the relationship between ecology and development. By doing so he, as a Dalit writer, urges his readers to at least reflect on them. This is what Dalit aesthetics is all about. As Sharankumar Limbale writes, 'The aesthetics of Dalit literature rests on: first, the artists' social commitment; second, the life-affirming values present in the artistic creation and third, the ability to raise the reader's consciousness of fundamental values like equality, freedom, justice and fraternity' (120). It will not be an exaggeration to say that Akhila Naik's *Bheda* has successfully dealt with all three aspects of Dalit literature that Limbale has referred to.

Ernst Fischer in his book *The Necessity of Art: A Marxist Approach* (1963) wrote that the purpose of art or literature cannot be merely aesthetic; there has to be a certain moral and social concern to it as well. Though writers cannot always actually bring about changes in society they can at least help create awareness. Even if they cannot offer solutions to problems, they can at least diagnose the disease. Avrom Fleishman has this to say on the function of literature:

> Literature supplements not only the primary cultural world of language, belief, and behavior but second-level systems as well, which like it attempt to discourse of those discourses. As in the human sciences, which have been shown to operate by conceptual schemes tantamount to fictions, the role of literary functions is to locate us in our human world, to contrive for us a securer perch in reality by all the arts at its disposal. To determine how literature does this, by comparison with the fictions by which the human sciences confront reality, will help us toward the special virtue of fiction as a genre, toward its supplementary and invaluable contribution to the cultural world. . . . (13)

Thus, literature goes beyond being a historical record; it is an imaginative representation of human experience and so long as it has the power to question our unthinking assumptions, it has contributed to the human cause. Dalit writers like Akhila Naik certainly approach literature from this direction.

REFERENCES

Clark, T. W. *The Novel in India: Its Birth and Development*. London: George Allen and Unwin, 1970. Print.

Deo, Fanindam. *Roots of Poverty: A Social History*. Bhubaneswar: Amadeus Press, 2009. Print.

Devi, Vidya. *Dalit and Social Justice*. New Delhi: MD Publications, 2008. Print.

Fischer, Ernst. *The Necessity of Art: A Marxist Approach*. 1963. London: Verso Reprint, 2010. Print.

Fleishman, Avrom. *Fiction and the Ways of Knowing*. Austin: U of Texas P, 1978. Print.

Gajarawala, Toral Jatin. *Untouchable Fictions: Literary Realism and the Crisis of Caste*. New York: Fordham UP, 2013. Print.

Kumar, Raj. 'Caste and the Literary Imagination in the Context of Odia Literature: A Reading of Akhila Naik's *Bheda*'. *Dalit Literatures in India.* Eds. Judith Misrahi-Barak and Joshil K. Abraham. New Delhi: Routledge, 2016. Print.

Kumar, Raj. Translator's Note. *Bheda*. By Akhila Naik. Trans. Raj Kumar. New Delhi: Oxford UP, 2017. Print.

Limbale, Sharankumar. *Towards an Aesthetic of Dalit Literature: History, Controversies and Consideration*. Trans. Alok Mukherjee. New Delhi: Orient BlackSwan, 2010. Print.

Macwan, Joseph. *Angaliyat: The Stepchild*. Trans. Rita Kothari. New Delhi: Oxford UP, 2004. Print.

Mukherjee, Meenakshi, ed. *Early Novels in India*. New Delhi: Sahitya Akademi, 2010. Print.

Naik, Akhila. *Bheda*. Trans. Raj Kumar. New Delhi: Oxford UP, 2017. Print.

Rao, G. Kalyan. *Untouchable Spring*. Trans. Alladi Uma and M. Sridhar. New Delhi: Orient BlackSwan, 2010. Print.

Rao, Yagati Chinna. *Presidential Address to Andhra Pradesh History Congress*. Guntur, 23-24, February, 2010.

Sivakami, P. *The Grip of Change*, Chennai: Orient Longman, 2006. Print.

Chapter Six

Pedagogical Approaches to Dalit Literature

Modern Dalit literature is already forty-five years old, if we consider the launch of a literary movement by the Dalit Panthers in Maharashtra in 1972 as its foundational moment. Currently Dalit writing can be found in almost all Indian languages. Dalit literature is also being translated into many Indian languages as well as English, and is being taken up seriously by globally renowned publishers. Apart from being available to general readership, Dalit literature is now a part of the curricula in schools, colleges and universities in India and abroad. This leads Gopal Guru, a theoretician and social scientist, to comment,

> The public imagination in India seems to be increasingly gripped with Dalit issues and concerns. This is evident in the writings of both Dalits and non-Dalits, who have focused on a variety of Dalit issues ranging from theory to poetry. Books on Dalit themes now find nominal accommodation in some of the leading publishing houses in India. Dalit issues previously did not receive much recognition from those who had complete control over the sphere of critical public inquiry, but that group has now found the issues worthy of scholarly attention. Prior to the 1990s, continuous marginalization and ghettoization implicitly suggested that the so-called Dalit question failed to attract any serious attention from the intellectual mainstream. Thus it is rather gratifying to note that Dalit studies, though previously present at various levels, are now ending this silence and have begun receiving

> far more serious intellectual attention from the national and international scholarly communities. (31)

Before the 90s, Dalits were considered to be the 'others' in Indian caste society. This 'othering of others' took place everywhere for the Dalits, be it in government policies, academic institutions, administrations or in larger civil society. In 1991–92, the Central Government, under V. P. Singh, celebrated Ambedkar's birth centenary as the year of social justice and undertook several measures which helped Dalits to become a part of civil society. In order to propound and propagate Ambedkar's philosophy, his writings and speeches were published in English and were later translated into Indian languages. Ambedkar Chairs were established in universities to facilitate research on Dalit issues and literature. Reservations in government jobs took effect. It is against this background that Arjun Dangle's edited anthology, *Poisoned Bread: Translations from Modern Marathi Dalit Literature*, the first English translation of modern Marathi Dalit writings, came out in 1992. This was the first ever such anthology in English and helped the non-Marathi speaking public to read Marathi Dalit literature. Once access to writings in this area as well as general consciousness about Dalit contexts grew, students and teachers from several universities, both within India and abroad, took up research on Dalit-related subjects. All this led to the emergence of the discipline called Dalit studies in the 1990s.

Like gender studies or cultural studies, Dalit studies has now been established as a full-fledged autonomous discipline in colleges and universities. Apart from literature, subjects such as history, political science, economics, sociology, psychology, philosophy and law are affiliated with Dalit studies. Unfortunately, the number of institutions offering Dalit studies or courses on Dalit issues in India is very few. There are many reasons why several universities have not included Dalit studies in their curricula. It may be that they are uncomfortable with it because as a discipline it raises questions around Dalit subalterns and the ethical and moral responsibilities of Indian upper-caste citizens. However, those universities which already have Dalit studies face many challenges in terms of students' enrolment, infrastructural facilities, questions over pedagogical approaches, etc., among other issues. So, what is the future of Dalit literature? How is it doing as a discipline? Who teaches it? What are some of the pedagogical approaches to Dalit literature? These are the questions this chapter will try to address.

ENGLISH IN THE DALIT CONTEXT

In 1835, Macaulay's 'Minute' made the English language the medium for higher education in India. Macaulay's intention was to create an official class that was 'Indian in blood and colour, but English in taste, in opinions, in morals, and intellect'. Thus, a new hierarchy was established where competence in English would be a crucial factor in determining economic security and social status.

The new opportunity was grabbed largely by those who were already at the top of the traditional social structure. Thus, the upper castes, who had easy access to higher education in the new dispensation, also obtained better jobs in the British administration. The lower castes, on the other hand, could not reap much benefit from the British educational policy, because they could not avail of education due to the structural and social inequalities perpetrated by the caste system.

Another effect was that brahmins and other upper castes were appointed by the British to translate the bulk of the old Sanskrit law books to be used as guides in the formation of the colonial judicial system. It is said that Sir William Jones, a judge of the Supreme Court and the founder of the Asiatic Society, used to discuss Sanskrit manuscripts with pundits. The learned judge felt so much enthusiasm for these brahminical ideas and texts that he himself translated the *Manusmriti* into English. Later, he also translated some Indian classical texts including Kalidasa's *Abhijñānaśhākuntalam*. Thus, the literary and intellectual activities of the early English administrators and judges only further reinforced the brahminical hierarchies of the caste system. Gauri Viswanathan comments on the deeper effects of the introduction of English education in India:

> English education, fighting to stave off the appearance of imposing an alien culture on native society, gained subtle redefinition as an instrument of authenticity. A historical consciousness was intended to bring the Indian in touch with

> himself, recovering his true essence and identity from the degradation to which it had become subject through native despotism. Far from alienating the Indian from his own culture, background, and traditions, English education gained the image of being an agency for restoring Indian youth to an essential self and, in turn, reinserting him into the course of Western civilization. (134)

In all this, Dalits, women and members of other lower caste communities remained unable to access any form of education, despite the intense interventions of Christian missionaries.

Jotiba Phule and his wife Savitribai Phule were the first Indian couple to start teaching Dalit boys and girls in their schools. For such bold acts the Phules were ex-communicated from their family. All the non-brahmin leaders – Phule, Ambedkar and Periyar, among others – emphasised the importance of education. After independence, the Indian Constitution made provisions for compulsory education for all. Yet, social exclusion has ensured that Dalits have remained economically, socially and educationally backward. Since they are poor, a very small percentage of them have gained access to English education. English is one of the most sought-after languages in the globalised world, and so Dalit writers and activists feel that Dalits should avail of English education as it can only be to their advantage. Mogalli Ganesh, a Kannada Dalit writer and activist, for example, observes that it is the English language that will give Dalits that opportunity to liberate themselves:

> For marginalized communities the only access to education has been through modernity. In spite of its late arrival, the awareness it has created has been momentous. English education, by showing the Dalits a glimpse of the wider world, pointed to a new possibility of liberation. . . . What was a weapon of the state and the means of colonial exploitation was a boon as far as the Dalits were concerned. Brahmanical communities have used modern English education for their cultural revival. The lower castes have avoided this and their quest has been different. . . . For whom is English, and globalization shaped by English, harmful? Ambedkar's success in fashioning a vocabulary of liberation for the Dalits, in English, is one of the most significant milestones of the century. . . . The fact

> that English destroys native languages should be juxtaposed with the fact that it is the Dalits who need English the most. In fact, Dalits should be given English education as a matter of priority. (65–67)

Ganesh's observation is a valid one because in a globalised and highly competitive world knowledge and mastery of English can help one get a non-menial job. English is also considered to be a language of liberation because unlike Indian languages, which are inherently casteist, English is relatively 'caste neutral'. One of the best examples of this is Mulk Raj Anand's first novel *Untouchable* which refers to Dalit communities in general and does not name any particular Dalit community such as bhangi, mala, madiga or mahar. Each of these names denotes a particular and demeaning occupational status in a caste society. Other than that, these groups have no other identity. It is in this sense that the term 'untouchable', as compared to bhangi, mala, madiga or mahar, is in many ways neutral because it does not suggest any particular traditional occupation of a Dalit community.

But there are also contrasting opinions regarding English education among Dalits. M. Dasan, a Dalit intellectual and activist, for example, thinks that English, being the language of the rulers, is hegemonic and therefore discriminates between its recipients, particularly those who are at the margins. Moreover, he feels that English education will bring about homogeneity among different social groups which may finally suppress and marginalise the diversities that characterise Dalit cultures and languages:

> In India, the English curriculum continues to remain a means of control over, and distribution of, social and intellectual capital. The current usage and imposition of English in most global situations replay hegemonic colonial relations, and this requires greater critical enquiry. The English curriculum is used to discriminate between individuals in terms of mastery, fluency and competency. The undue importance given to the English language results in suppression and marginalization of the diverse historical values and attitudes that various indigenous languages and literature could have imbued the younger generation with. Teaching only those traditions valued by the mainstream entrenches certain discursive

> practices while marginalizing others, without examining the assumptions that underpin them. (55–56)

Dasan believes that even if Dalits are educated in English and are well-placed in the job market, they are never free from caste oppression. This means that English education for Dalits will not solve their caste problems:

> In fact, many of the English-educated Dalits have become Dalit elites, and have been able to negotiate power with the bureaucracy and political leadership. The knowledge of English has also enhanced employment opportunities, which in turn have increased their income levels and social status. Now, they not only know how to curse the oppressors, but also how to articulate their voices in a better and stronger way to a large audience (both national and international). Yet, despite their improved ability and proficiency in the English language, they are still discriminated against. So I doubt the efficacy/credibility of the simplistic argument that proficiency in English can do away with the inherent vices in the Brahminical social order – which is primarily responsible for the inferior status of the Dalit masses – and can put an end to Dalit suffering(s). I feel that we should also take into consideration the social, cultural, political, and economic dimensions of Dalits while discussing the question of Dalits and English in India. Arguing for Englishing Dalits as the only way to liberate and empower them would be too reductive. (56)

This project of 'Englishing Dalits' was strongly advocated by Chandra Bhan Prasad, a Delhi-based Dalit intellectual, in 2004 when he hosted a birthday party in honour of Thomas Babington Macaulay. He also published an article titled 'Reinventing Lord Macaulay' where he termed Macaulay as 'the finest rationalist of his time' for introducing English in India. In the same article Prasad also opined that 'English is the only agency that can connect people around the globe to the Dalit experience' (1). This was followed by the inauguration of a temple in Bankagaon, in Lakhimpur Kheri district, Uttar Pradesh, on 30 April 2010, dedicated to the Dalit 'Goddess English'. A thirty-inch bronze idol, sculpted by artist Shanti Swaroop Baudh, was installed in the temple. The icon is modelled on the Statue of Liberty and has some distinct features. The Goddess is perched atop a computer, and holds a pen in her raised right hand and books in her lowered left hand. She has also a *burra sahib*-like floppy hat upon her head. This installation of English as a goddess seems to be sending a message: English has become the language of survival and decolonisation for Dalits. Yet Kancha Ilaiah has this to say about his own experiences with language (English and Telugu) in school:

> What difference did it make to us whether we had an English textbook that talked about Milton's *Paradise Lost* or *Paradise Regained*, or Shakespeare's *Othello* or *Macbeth* or Wordsworth's poetry about nature in England, or a Telugu textbook which talked about Kalidasa's *Meghasandesham*, Bommera Potanna's *Bhagavatam*, or Nannaya and Tikkana's *Mahabharatham* except the fact that one textbook is written with twenty-six letters and the other in fifty-six letters? We do not share the contents of either; we do not find our lives reflected in their narratives. We cannot locate our family settings in them. In none of these books do we find words that are familiar to us. Without the help of a dictionary neither makes any sense to us. How does it make any difference to us whether it is Greek and Latin that are written in Roman letters or Sanskrit that is written in Telugu? (15)

Ilaiah's observation is important because the language used in school textbooks is usually never inclusive as the government-appointed textbook committee members more often than not belong to the upper castes, who see to it that the language used in textbooks is often the official, Sanskritised version (especially Indian languages). They usually do not take into account whether children from Dalit, Adivasi and lower-caste communities are comfortable with such a highly structured and standardised language. Ilaiah's solution is that instead of imposing a foreign tongue (English), the government should evolve a system whereby the people's language can be used in textbook writing. Of course, given the fact that India is a multi-lingual, multi-cultural, multi-ethnic, multi-religious country, any debate on which languages to use will be difficult to resolve. One can only expect that the policymakers responsible for selecting languages for different purposes are sensible and sensitive enough to address the various issues faced by people belonging to various strata of society.

LITERARY STUDIES IN INDIA

Dalit literature is a new literature in terms of its themes, language, structure and pedagogy. Since it is now offered as a course in universities, it comes under the purview of literary studies.

Literary studies in India can be traced back to 1857, when the universities of Bombay, Madras and Calcutta were established. At the time, fixed sets of syllabi were followed along the pattern of the University of London. While conventional grammar became an important component of the language paper, the English literature in the university syllabus was mostly confined to canonised English texts. The papers in English literature generally began with the writings of Geoffrey Chaucer and ended with T. S. Eliot. Gauri Viswanathan (1989), Svati Joshi (1991), Rajeshwari Sunder Rajan (1992), Susie Tharu (1998), Alok Mukherjee (2009) and others have attempted to bring out many fascinating and problematic facets about the history and practice of reading and teaching literature in India. Viswanathan, in her path-breaking book *Masks of Conquest*, for example, reveals how, with the introduction of the English language, the British government tried to bring about a standardisation of the otherwise heterogeneous Indian educational system:

> As a time capsule for English culture, India provided an ideal setting. The structure of Indian society, its multiple languages and multiple religions, eliminated some of the chief difficulties encountered in England in the preservation of a pure national culture. For the differentiated education that the Indian social structure encouraged – vernaculars for the lower castes and the classical languages of Arabic, Sanskrit, and Persian for the upper classes of Hindus and Muslims – minimized the possibilities of one language ever achieving the status of common language for all the population. Linguistic stratification of classes permitted English high culture to be maintained in all its purity without erosion that was occurring to polite literature in England. The resistance of the English language to standardization of use in England is a measure

> of the problematic control of linguistic and literary forms wherever English, as a living language of daily speech and communication shared by a wide public, is used and produced outside institutional controls such as, for example, formal education. (116)

This pattern was followed all over India and continued for several decades even after Indian independence. Interestingly, the people who were involved in the preservation and continuation of English literary studies in India after independence were mostly upper-caste brahmin men. With degrees from Oxford or Cambridge, they carried forward the baggage of colonialism and ensured that the day-to-day functioning of the Indian university system became a peculiar form of caste prejudice. English language became the 'holy cow' and only the 'sacred' brahmin teachers were recruited to teach English literature. English departments continued to function within the caste matrix for several years and were slow to change; it is only several decades later that the lower castes and Dalits entered the university system as faculty members by availing of the reservation system.

After independence, socio-political movements changed many aspects of the nation, and higher education was no exception. Today the syllabus of English literature is no longer dominated by British literature. Components of Indian literature, American literature, contemporary literature, film studies, gender studies, Dalit studies, translation studies, language theories, etc., are also included. This development is part of a project that has sought to make English literature truly 'interdisciplinary' in character. Also, the teachers of English literature are no longer brahmins alone. Thanks to the protective discrimination policy enshrined in the Indian Constitution, today Dalits, Adivasis, people from Other Backward Classes and women have become English teachers. But this does not necessarily mean that English literature departments in Indian universities have become truly 'inclusive'. These are often only 'token' gestures made to address the idea of social justice. Some of the other common problems we regularly encounter while teaching English literature across universities are: inadequate classrooms and lack of infrastructural facilities such as books, journals and libraries, and uneven student–teacher ratio. There are indications that the teaching–learning standard in schools and colleges is going down. This will surely have an impact on the success of teaching–learning methods in higher educational institutions.

Susie Tharu, while reviewing the teaching of English literature in the nineties, cautions us about the politics and history of literary studies in India:

> Obviously the politics and history of English in India, and the politics and history of literary studies, cannot just be "set aside" any more than ex-colonial peoples can set aside their cringe or women can set aside the ideologies that subjugate them. Consider, as one instance, the master-subjectivity that has been nurtured and endorsed by literary studies. The subtle historical structuring of that subjectivity, its commitments – bourgeois-nationalist, patriarchal, colonial, but also as a quite evident today, upper-caste and orientalist Hindu – its designs for identity, its anxieties about alienation, and its desires, sit uneasy on the subject positions available for habitation. There is no legitimate space in a world designed to house this subject for the many struggles against oppression and expropriation and the many aspirations for freedom that comprise our history and our politics. The interests and the orientation of this master-subjectivity are often in radical conflict with those with which as women, workers, Muslims, peasants, lower castes, black and colonial peoples generally, we struggle to live at the edges of its world. It must be obvious that major problems will arise when we continue today to regard this subjectivity and its "humanism" as natural, and take its contours for granted as we force our students to "awaken" into its life. (27–28)

The 'alienation' that Tharu has pointed out in the paragraph above still exists. It is true that education is available for Dalits, but caste discrimination persists in all educational institutions – school, college or university. While the majority of Dalit children drop out of school, the few who persevere and enter higher education have to face caste discrimination. With the advent of globalisation in the 1990s, higher education in India is being reshaped, as more and more foreign universities have been setting up campuses in India. Within India, too, private universities have mushroomed, as big businesses (mostly owned by upper castes) have found higher education to be a lucrative business venture. With competition all around, state and local universities suffer from a resource crunch, lacking infrastructure and faculty strength. On the other hand, private agencies and educational institutions seem to be unnecessarily interfering in the smooth functioning of higher education. In '"Globalization", Culture and the University', Masao Miyoshi, Professor of Comparative Literature at UC San Diego, draws on his own and his colleagues' experiences and argues that

> The state has lost power to transnational corporations, which have begun to determine university politics. From their point of view, cultural productions are profitable commodities to be marketed, and it is the task of the university to transform their academic programmes accordingly. To serve their purposes, parameters to be introduced, like course enrolment, student-teacher ratio or the number of majors in a department, are to be geared towards a system of ranking, which in turn establishes the reputation of a university and the value of its products in a competitive national and international market. (Riemenschneider 99)

Miyoshi also goes on to say that, 'Excellence is to be achieved for the sake of excellence, and professors who once presumably professed . . . are now merely professionals, entrepreneurs, careerists, and opportunists, as in the corporate world' (99).

What we have witnessed in the recent times is that while departments such as economics, commerce and the sciences have gained a lot from the privatisation of the Indian economy, particularly in terms of employment opportunities, the humanities and social sciences have suffered badly. How will a course like Dalit studies, which is comparatively new, going to survive in this market-driven environment? Will it be able to effect real social change?

DALIT STUDIES IN INDIA: CONTEXT AND APPROACHES

When Dalit studies was first introduced in Indian universities, it was a 'shock' to many upper-caste academics because they would have liked to maintain the status quo both in curricula and methodologies.

Dalit studies as a discipline requires ethical and moral discussions on the caste questions. Would upper-caste teachers and students feel comfortable if questions around caste are raised in classrooms? Given the social background of the majority of teachers, students and the pedagogical approaches used for the teaching–learning processes, one can easily understand why the majority of Indian universities were and still are not ready to embrace new subjects and methodologies. It is a rather difficult proposition for upper-caste teachers and students to discuss and debate Dalit rights and freedom in classrooms without interrogating themselves. To do this they have to surrender their 'communal ego' and embrace a new position of being 'democratic' and 'inclusive'. But doing so is difficult because, to listen to the voices of the 'unspeakable' and bring those voices into academic sphere we need to have what Gayatri Chakravorty Spivak calls 'radical alterity'. Only then can we listen to the voices of others:

> Radical alterity – the wholly other – must be thought through imagining. To be born human is to be born angled toward an other and others. To account for this, the human being presupposes the 'quite-other'. This is the bottomline of being-human as being-in-the ethical relation. By definition we cannot – no self can – reach the 'quite-other'. . . . This is the founding gap in all acts or talk, most especially in acts or talk we understand to be closest to the ethical – the historical and political. We must somehow attempt to supplement the gap. (Spivak 98)

Given the kind of historical and political role played by the upper castes in Indian society, any kind of radical debate on either Dalits or caste in Indian universities seems next to impossible. This does not mean that there is no debate on caste in Indian academia. Since the Mandal Commission recommendations in 1992, most Indian universities have witnessed debates on caste politics. In recent times one can see more debates on caste-related issues taking place in many Indian universities such as Jawaharlal Nehru University, the University of Delhi and the University of Hyderabad. But the caste debates conducted in most Indian universities are mostly at a superficial level, concerned more with rhetoric and slogan-shouting.

No one really talks about bringing changes at the structural level where Dalits also can participate in the decision-making process of the university system.

There have been some changes in Indian universities in recent times. Apart from giving admission to students from Dalit, Adivasi and Other Backward Class (OBC) communities, universities across India are recruiting teachers from these communities as a result of the enforcement of reservation as provided in the Constitution. As a result, there is growing diversity in Indian universities. The classrooms are now a mix of students coming from all social strata. Teachers, especially those from Dalit, Adivasi and OBC backgrounds, bring their social experiences to classroom teaching. This was not possible a few years back. Meenakshi Mukherjee, in her article 'English in an Uneven World', recounts the way Indian academia used to deliberately ignore the presence of Dalit literature: 'When we discussed Indian Writing in English, in the classroom or in academic seminars, no reference was ever made to Dalit writing. It was automatically assumed that Bakha would never have a voice in English without the mediation of a London-educated Mulk Raj Anand' (18).

DALIT STUDIES AND DALIT POLITICS OF EMANCIPATION

Dalit literature comes from the margins and questions the ideas of equality, justice and dignity in Indian society. By identifying 'caste' as the main problem of Indian society, Dalit literature addresses the idea of liberation from caste slavery. In this context, one is reminded of the 'philosophy of liberation' once propounded by the Latin American philosopher Enrique Dussel. He observes,

> Philosophy of liberation is a pedagogical activity stemming from a praxis that roots itself in proximity of teacher-pupil, thinker-pupil. Although pedagogical, it is a praxis conditioned by political (and erotic) praxis. Nevertheless, as pedagogical, its essence is theoretical and speculative. Theoretical action, the poetic intellectual illuminative activity of the philosopher, sets out to discover and expose (in the exposition and risk of the life of the philosopher), in the presence of an entrenched system,

> all moments of negation and all exteriority lacking justice. For this reason it is an analectical pedagogy of liberation. That is, it is the magisterium that functions in the name of the poor, the oppressed, the other, the one who like a hostage within the system testifies to the fetishism of its totalization and predicts its death in the liberating action of the dominated. (178)

True to Dussel's observations, Dalits in India are doomed by caste. From the time they are born, they are subjected to caste humiliations. Even after their death, the 'untouchable' ghost continues to haunt them. Therefore, when they are alive, they write poetry and autobiographies to record their lived experiences. But their writings must be read in a larger context because they are nothing but a cry for freedom. This is what the Indian philosopher Sundar Sarukkai believes when he writes,

> Suppose we say that to be a Dalit subject is to be oppressed with no choice of escaping this oppression. Then the lived experience of Dalits is not about sharing their lifestyles, living with them, and being like them, but *being them* in the sense that you *cannot* be anything else. Or, in other words, to be a Dalit is not to share all that they have but to share what they cannot have. Lived experience is not about what there is but is about what there is not. *Lived experience is not about freedom of experience but about the lack of freedom in an experience.* (Emphasis in original, Guru and Sarukkai 36)

If Dalit literature is a cry for freedom, how does one understand and interpret its language? Compared to Indian literature, Dalit literature is distinct and different in more than one way. Since Dalit literature originates from a certain political commitment of the author, we must try to understand the way a Dalit text performs radical politics. And behind this radical politics, there is a whole background of lived reality Dalit writers have to represent in their writings. This leads Laura R. Brueck to observe that 'modern Dalit literature in fact exhibits a nuanced treatment of literary language and an intentional approach to narrative form that not only deserves close critical attention but that also allows for a more careful understanding of the interstices of Dalit activism, "consciousness", and literary expression' (8).

To understand Dalit literary activism one has to situate Dalit writings in a historical context. Since caste is the main target, the poetics and politics of Dalit writings ultimately are directed towards the question of how to annihilate caste. And to achieve this, Dalit writers have to negotiate between political rhetoric and radical alternatives. The political rhetoric is to bring an end to the everyday life of caste and the radical alternative is to live in a casteless society. If this is the kind of project Dalit writers are engaged in, then Dalit texts demand a complex reading and pedagogical approach. Toral Jatin Gajarawala observes,

> Dalit texts, like many other texts, contain elements of the traditionally realist and the utopian, the magical, the pedagogical. But they rhetorically insist on the reading of those elements within the framework of a realist epistemology rather than their narrative sequestering as subjectivist, fabulist, "agitational" or "prescriptive." To agree to this would be to grant to the Dalit realist text the privileges the realist text has accrued elsewhere. The Dalit text has to be necessarily concerned with caste status as immutable and fixed, as well as with its transcendence, without which the Dalit text could not be. This is less utopian or melodramatic than it is the product of a modern subjectivity. Dalit writing, reorganizing the world according to caste, is using the old categories of realist referentiality to make certain political claims, the elaboration of which require triangulation, circumvention, bifurcation. (19–20)

Since Dalit writers' approach to caste is based on their social experiences, Dalit writings must be read along with other disciplines. Therefore, reading Dalit literature demands an interdisciplinary approach. Teaching Dalit studies will definitely demand looking at Indian culture, civilisation, history, language, religion and literature from a new perspective. This may not be easy because the current understanding of these subjects is mostly traditional and not critical. So what kind of critical pedagogical practice can be used to re-understand these subjects? Rita Felski in *Uses of Literature* has emphasised how shock is a novelty in any modern criticism:

> When a new form or genre appears on the scene, its effect is to render the ordinary strange, to challenge our usual ways of

> seeing, to startle us out of the torpor of habitual perceptions and received ideas. In altering how we see, it also changes what we see. Yet this effect, by its nature, can only be finite and short-lived. Shock is gradually drained of its emotive impact and power to change consciousness. Disorientation gives way to eventual acceptance as once puzzling or bizarre forms of expression are gradually absorbed into our cultural lexicon. The history of literature is thus driven by an endless spiral of surprise-habituation-surprise, as established styles yield to new techniques that can again revitalize perception. (114–15)

True to Felski's observation, the presence of Dalit literature was initially ignored by the establishment. Later, upper-caste critics went to the extent of terming it propagandist literature. They also condemned Dalit writers' choice of literary forms, languages and aesthetics. Today the 'shock' is almost over because Dalit literature is now a part of almost every Indian university curricula. So the first and foremost challenge is how to situate Dalit texts in their proper contexts so that the Dalit vision of the text is not lost. The Dalit vision of emancipation is often misunderstood by many. Since there are hundreds of Dalit communities across India with different religions, languages, customs and conventions, critics argue that there cannot be a single Dalit vision. The first and foremost agenda of the Dalit vision is the annihilation of caste. Since caste as a social system prevents Dalits from having dignity and self-respect, Dalit writers work hard to restore their lost selves through a new language. Therefore, on the surface it seems that Dalit writing is calling for a new identity. But this is only partially true. Dalit identity has to be broadly understood as a new subjectivity. Crushed by caste rules for long, Dalit subjectivity is only now somewhat free to narrate its caste experience with a newly acquired language. Behind these narratives, there is a rejection of the old identity for a new one. The old identity is the 'untouchable' past and the new one incorporates the idea of dignity and self-respect as opposed to the Hindu idea of rejection and humiliation. Thus, Dalit identity is also a political praxis that calls for the freedom of the Dalit masses. If we do not take this into account, we may not be able to understand the emancipation project that informs Dalit writing. As Arun Kumar, the Dalit critic, warns us, 'Denuding dalit writings of its political tenor and reducing it merely to cultural concerns for identity would be a failure in evaluating the works being produced since the late 1960s. It will limit the dalit political agenda by eclipsing the vision for a comprehensive change' (3).

Teachers and students of Dalit studies must be sensitive to the various social and cultural practices of the language community whose linguistic and literary practices they are studying. Since language is culture, Dalit language has to be read with reference to everyday Dalit cultural practices. Hindu culture kept Dalit culture at a safe distance. This compelled Dalits to take a critical position against Hindu culture and critique its position and power, especially through language. Evidence suggests that there exists a certain Dalit vocabulary which has developed over time as a response to, as criticism and mockery of, brahminism. Gail Omvedt points out,

> In nearly all Indian languages today, crucial differences of vocabulary and pronunciation continue to function along caste lines; they work as means of caste differentiation and as ways of reproducing caste. For children from Shudra and Dalit backgrounds are constantly faced with the perception that "they don't speak right." To take just one minor example, "Brahman" is pronounced "bahman" in the Bahujan-Dalit forms of almost every language – this is considered insulting, but in fact it reflects a social reality that goes back thousand years. In the Prakrit also, it was invariably "bahman". (23)

For a person the choice of a language mostly comes from his/her social location. Since a language is always acquired, the immediate social environment of the person is largely responsible for acquisition of that language. In the case of Dalit language, we have already discussed how Dalits inherit the language of the communities to which they belong. Since it is caste that gives a language the power to dominate, Dalit language is considered 'low' by the upper castes. In such a scenario, Dalits have no choice but to acquire a few non-Dalit languages, apart from their own, to communicate with others. The Dalit literary use of language has to be understood in this larger context.

Since Dalit lives are intrinsically related to several aspects of Indian society, the teaching of Dalit literature requires exposure to various disciplines such as history, sociology, philosophy, religion, law, etc., apart from language and literature. This may pose a challenge to teachers of Dalit literature. Teachers teaching Dalit literature must have a proper understanding of Dalit lives, culture, religion and language, among other subjects. An understanding of such multiple subjects certainly needs some kind of social and political commitment by both teachers and students. Otherwise, the context of Dalit literature will be lost. S. H. Olsen, a literary critic, talks about this:

> Literature is a social practice not merely in the minimal sense that it involves a group of people among whom literary works are produced and read, but also in the stricter sense that it is a practice whose existence depends on a background of concepts and conventions which create the possibility of identifying literary works and provide a framework for appreciation, and on the people actually applying these concepts and conventions in their approach to literary works. . . . A literary work must . . . be seen as being offered to an audience by an author with the intention that it should be understood with reference to a shared background of concepts and conventions which must be employed to determine its aesthetic features. A reader must be conceived of as a person who approaches the work with a set of expectations defined in terms of these concepts and conventions. Somebody who did not share this institutional background would not be able to identify aesthetic features in it because he did not know the concepts and conventions which define these features. (533)

If liberty, dignity and equality for all is the proposition Dalit writers are making, it is also equally important to understand the way Dalit literature has given voice to the voiceless. Judging by the Dalit writers' use of new vocabularies, I believe one can look forward to Dalit literary practices gradually bringing about social changes in India. As we have already discussed, Dalit literature is not about the literary expression of a few educated Dalit writers and activists; it is about Dalit collectives who are hoping to live a dignified life in India. Turning such high hopes into reality needs some concrete plan of action from below. To see such action come to fruition means bringing about praxis both in the classroom as well as outside. Peniel Rajkumar, who has studied Dalit theology and liberation in depth, has made the following observations in terms of such praxis:

> In praxiological terms, this aspect of conflict and confrontation can be understood as conscientious resistance to oppression and injustice. As praxis involves a dialectic between action and reflection, the component of pedagogy can function as reflection – the part where people are enabled to reflect upon their actions. This critical dimension of praxis can be translated into concrete and corporate action when it is revalidated as pedagogy for a wider group. This feature of conflict/confrontation involves justice as action, which involves resisting actions which dehumanize. It also includes critical retrospection of the ethical validity of human modes of structuring "order". (106)

This means that the upper castes need to change their perceptions and imaginations, particularly about Dalits. Only then will they be able to appreciate Dalit creativity. Before they dismiss the entire philosophy of Dalit literature, they must patiently listen to the voices coming from the margins. That is the first and most important restructuring of 'order' that needs to happen for members of caste society. The day they can understand the reasons why Dalits demand dignity and self-respect will be the beginning of the end of the caste system. This is how the entire pedagogical approach to Dalit studies needs to be oriented.

CONCLUSION

Since the relationship between caste and Dalit lives is very complex, Dalit literature must be read with all its complexities intact. Dalit texts are dynamic by nature and readers/interpreters must take cognisance of their dynamism. Before entering into the logic of any Dalit text, it is important to know the historical past of Dalit communities so that we know the realities of Dalit lives. Dalit texts must be put into their proper contexts; otherwise, the Dalit vision will be lost. This is the challenge in understanding Dalit texts and more importantly, Dalit lives.

REFERENCES

Brueck, Laura R. *Writing Resistance: The Rhetorical Imagination of Hindi Dalit Literature*. New York: Columbia UP, 2014. Print.

Dasan, M. 'Englishing Dalits: Problems and Perspectives'. *English in the Dalit Context*. Eds. Alladi Uma, et al. New Delhi: Orient BlackSwan, 2014. 51–61. Print.

Dussel, Enrique. *Philosophy of Liberation*. Trans. Aquilina Martinez and Christine Morkovsky. New York: Orbis, 1985. Print.

Felski, Rita. *Uses of Literature*. Blackwell: United Kingdom, 2008. Print.

Gajarawala, Toral Jatin. *Untouchable Fictions: Literary Realism and the Crisis of Caste*. New York: Fordham UP, 2013. Print.

Ganesh, Mogalli. *Dalitaru mattu jagatikarana*. Trans. Rajendra Chenni. Hampi: Kannada University, 1998. Translated and quoted in 'Struggles over the Sign: Discourses on English' by Rajendra Chenni and included in Uma, Alladi et al., ed. *English in the Dalit Context*. New Delhi: Orient BlackSwan, 2014. Print.

Guru, Gopal. 'The Indian Nation in Its Egalitarian Conception'. *Dalit Studies*. Ed. S. Ramnarayan and K. Satyanarayana. Ranikhet: Permanent Black, 2016. 31–49. Print.

Guru, Gopal, and Sundar Sarukkai. *The Cracked Mirror: An Indian Debate on Experience and Theory*. New Delhi: Oxford UP, 2012. Print.

Ilaiah, Kancha. *Why I am Not a Hindu: A Sudra Critique of Hindutva Philosophy, Culture and Political Economy*. Kolkata: Samya, 2012. Print.

Joshi, Svati, ed. *Re-Thinking English*. New Delhi: Trianka, 1991. Print.

Kumar, Arun. 'Introduction'. *Dalit Studies in Higher Education: Vision and Challenges*. Ed. Arun Kumar and Sanjay Kumar. New Delhi: Deshkal, 2005. 1–11. Print.

Mukherjee, Alok. *The Gift of English: English Education and the Formation of Alternative Hegemonies in India*. New Delhi: Orient BlackSwan, 2009. Print.

Mukherjee, Meenakshi. 'English in an Uneven Land, English in an Uneven World: Literature in English Translation'. *Southern Postcolonialisms: The Global South and the 'New' Literary Representations*. Ed. Sumanyu Satpathy. New Delhi: Routledge, 2009. 17–29. Print.

Olsen, S. H. 'Literary Aesthetics and Literary Practice.' *Mind* 90 (1981): 533. Print.

Omvedt, Gail. 'A Proposal for Dalit Studies'. *Dalit Studies in Higher Education: Vision and Challenges*. Ed. Arun Kumar and Sanjay Kumar. New Delhi: Deshkal, 2005. 17–25. Print.

Prasad, Chandra Bhan. 'Reinventing Lord Macaulay', *Countercurrents*, 27 October 2004. www.countercurrents.org/dalit-prasad271004.htm. Accessed 20 May 2018.

Rajkumar, Peniel. *Dalit Theology and Dalit Liberation: Problems, Paradigms and Possibilities*. Surrey: Ashgate, 2010. Print.

Riemenschneider, Dieter. 'The New English Language Literatures and the Globalization of Tertiary Education'. *Southern Postcolonialisms: The Global South and the 'New' Literary Representations*. Ed. Sumanyu Satpathy. New Delhi: Routledge, 2009. 97–110. Print.

Spivak, Gayatri Chakravorty. 'A Moral Dilemma'. *Can the Subaltern Speak?: Reflections on the History of an Idea*. Ed. Rosalind C. Morris. New York: Columbia UP, 2010. 21–78. Print.

Sunder Rajan, Rajeshwari. *The Lie of the Land*. New Delhi: Oxford UP, 1992. Print.

Tharu, Susie, ed. *Subject to Change: Teaching Literature in the Nineties*. Hyderabad: Orient Longman, 1998. Print.

Viswanathan, Gauri. *Masks of Conquest: Literary Study and British Rule in India*. New Delhi: Oxford UP, 1989. Print.

Conclusion

Modern Dalit literature is now more than five decades old. Over the years, Dalit writing has emerged in all genres and almost all Indian languages. Dalit literature has, therefore, now been established as a separate discipline in itself. However, literary criticism on Dalit literature is rare. The few books which are available are diverse in their themes and structures. The present book is a modest attempt to bridge this gap. It attempts to address all the major issues concerning Dalit literature in a single volume. Apart from literary criticism, the book also tries to introduce some important cultural concepts concerning Dalit communities.

'Dalit' is a name chosen by the 'untouchables' themselves, which implies self-pride as well as the marginal position in which they continue to live in Indian caste society. 'Dalit literature' can be defined as the literature written by Dalits. It reflects the Dalit consolidation of identity in Indian caste society, and their growing awareness and consciousness.

Dalits in India have been the victims of caste oppression for centuries. The caste system, based on 'purity' and 'pollution' norms, is primarily an invention of the upper castes to keep the lower castes under their control. Stringent caste laws were made to keep them poor and illiterate. Hindu Dharma shastras such as the *Manusmriti* were written to systematically deny them their civil and political rights. Since formal education was not available to them, Dalits could not think of launching a literary movement to narrate their oppressive lives and culture.

Like Indian society, Indian literature too was indifferent towards the plight of Dalits for a very long time. It is only at the beginning of the twentieth century that a few upper-caste Hindu writers attempted to portray the lives of the 'untouchables'. They tended to be driven either by zeal for social reform or by sentimental compassion. Unnava Lakshinarayana's *Malapalli* (Telugu, 1923), K. Shivaram Karanth's *Chomana dudi* (Kannada, 1933; *Choma's Drum*, 1978), Mulk Raj Anand's *Untouchable* (English, 1935), Thakazhi Sivasankara Pillai's *Thottiyude makan* (Malayalam, 1948; *Scavenger's Son*, 1994) and Gopinath Mohanty's *Harijan* (Odia, 1948) are a few Indian novels out of many where the main protagonists come from 'untouchable' communities. But the portrayal of these characters do not seem to be real; they are so idealised and portrayed as following the Hindu way of life that they can never be treated as ordinary human beings full of vitality, hope and despair.

Indian society has witnessed protests against the caste system from time to time, but the 'untouchables' do not seem to have gotten a reprieve from caste exploitation. The Buddha in the fourth century BCE and later many saint–poets like Chokhamela, Kabir, Nanak, Tukaram and others of the Bhakti movement (from the seventh to the seventeenth century AD) attacked caste practices and demanded equality and freedom for the lower strata of Indian society. Towards the end of the nineteenth century, protests against caste began more vigorously, led by the leaders of the non-brahmin movements. Jotibarao Phule, B. R. Ambedkar, Narayana Guru and Periyar were the prominent figures of these movements and put in immense efforts to fight against the caste system and untouchability in their own ways. They made efforts to educate Dalits, women and the lower castes. For example, in 1858, Phule opened a school for the children of 'untouchables' in Maharashtra – the first of its kind in India – thus striking at the root of caste hegemony. In 1873, he established the Satyashodhak Samaj, an organisation which proclaimed the need to save the lower castes from caste slavery. Later, Ambedkar led several movements for the social liberation, economic emancipation and political advancement of the downtrodden. He called for the annihilation of caste. He led the Dalit movement in Maharashtra for nearly three decades, which later spread all over India. He was the prime architect of the Indian Constitution which guaranteed every Indian citizen the right to liberty, equality and social justice. However, dismayed at the attitude of Indian caste society, Ambedkar, along with millions of his followers, converted to Buddhism in 1956, a few months before his death.

Ambedkar's movements resulted in bringing forth a consciousness among the educated Dalit youth of Maharashtra, who came together to launch an alternative literary and cultural movement. Accordingly, the first conference of Dalit writers was organized in Bombay in 1958 which went almost unnoticed by mainstream media. Thereafter, a number of Dalit writers made efforts to publish their works in little magazines such as *Fakta, Satyakatha*, *Kosala*, *Maratha*, *Marathwade*, etc. Upper-caste readers and reviewers rejected their writings, branding them as 'propagandist literature', and did not take them seriously. Dalit writers defended their positions with equal vigour. Later, Namdeo Dhasal, Arjun Dangle and J. V. Pawar took the initiative and established the Dalit Panthers in Bombay on 9 July 1972. The main objective of the Panthers was to create a counter culture, a separate identity for Dalits in society. This project was further articulated and spread by other Dalit writers, poets and activists through their writings and speeches. This led to the emergence of Dalit literature in Maharashtra in the 1970s, which subsequently spread to the neighbouring states of Gujarat, Karnataka, Andhra Pradesh and others.

Since the 1970s, an increasing number of poets and writers from Dalit communities in various Indian states have been producing literary works representing the themes of caste oppression, untouchability, poverty, repression and revolution. Their writings also contain powerful denunciations of and fierce attacks on the caste system and brahminical Hinduism. Dalit literature has brought diversity into modern Indian literature with the use of a separate Dalit language and Dalit discourse. There has also been an attempt on the part of Dalit writers to create a new aesthetics in their writings. Dalit literature has brought about a revolution in Indian literature and society where ex-'untouchables' are now using the traditionally denied weapon of literacy to expose the conditions under which they have lived, as well as to rebel against the Hindu institutions which have kept them in perpetual subordination.

Initially, Dalit writers wrote only poetry and autobiographies. They have subsequently experimented with and written in all genres such as novels, short stories, critical essays and plays. Many Dalit writers today write about gender-related issues, which had not been looked at previously. In fact, a number of Dalit women writers have written about their personal experiences, mostly critiquing the patriarchal social order that exists both outside of and within their communities. Thus, a paradigmatic shift is already visible with many Dalit writers raising their voices in a modern intersectional manner, against different forms of oppression related to class, gender, ethnicity, language, religion and other frameworks besides caste. More and more Dalit writings are now being translated into English and being published by well-known publishers. In the meantime, Dalit studies has been introduced as an academic discipline in several universities in India and abroad.

The book makes an attempt to address some of the major issues concerning Dalit literature. Several questions, such as, who is a Dalit, what is the philosophy of Dalit literature, what is Dalit aesthetics, how to approach Dalit literature, etc., have been explained with critical comments and references. The book also deals with Dalit life, culture and history in a major way as these areas inform Dalit literature and aesthetics. Apart from Dalit literary theory, the book has a chapter on Dalit critical practice where a Dalit novel has been critically analysed. Along with Dalit literary practices and Dalit studies, the book raises several questions about sociological and anthropological concepts such as class, ethnicity, language, region, religion, gender and nationalism, besides caste. Since it deals with such an array of subjects, the book covers more than what the title promises. It is hoped that it will help initiate dialogues on issues relating to Dalit life, dignity, self-respect and aesthetics.

Glossary of Select Terms

The purpose of this glossary is to give the reader a brief idea of some of the terms used in this book relating to Indian society in general and about Dalit language, culture and literature in particular.

Abhang: a form of devotional poetry sung in praise of Vithoba or Vitthala mostly by the Bhakti saint–poets of Maharashtra

Achhut: untouchable

Adivasi: a member of the aboriginal tribes of India

Angli: finger

Antyaja: untouchable; the literal meaning is 'end of birth' or 'last born'. According to Hindu laws, being 'untouchables', they can be born only once whereas the three upper-caste communities – brahmins, kshatriyas and vaishyas – are referred to as the 'twice-born'. The second 'birth' relates to initiation into structured education (of the Vedas and scriptures). This term therefore has implications for the denial of education and inability to rise through the ranks.

Arya or Aryan: a race of people who seem to have come to India from the Persian Gulf

Arya Samaj: a Hindu reform body started by Swami Dayanand Saraswati in 1875 in Maharashtra. As a part of their reform movement, the Arya Samajis distributed sacred threads among 'untouchables' to draw them into the caste-Hindu fold.

Ashrams: the four stages of a human life as described and prescribed in ancient Hindu texts – brahmacharya, grihastya, vanaprastha and sanyasa

Asiatic Society: a society founded by Sir William Jones on 15 January 1784 at Fort William in Calcutta (Kolkata), to further the cause of

Oriental research. It was initially named the 'Asiatick Society'. In 1825, it was renamed the Asiatic Society of Bengal.

***Asprushya*:** untouchable

***Ati-shudra*:** untouchable

***Avatar*:** incarnation of a god

***Bahishkrut*:** the excommunicated; those who are outside the fold of the Hindu caste system

***Bahman*:** same as 'brahman' or 'brahmin'

***Baniya*:** person belonging to the trader community

***Bhadralok*:** literally 'gentle man'; especially used in Bengal to describe a class of wealthy, well-educated people

Buddhism: a religion that encompasses a variety of traditions, beliefs and spiritual practices largely based on teachings attributed to the Buddha. It originated between the sixth and fourth centuries BCE. The Buddha was the first religious figure to oppose the caste system.

***Chaturvarna*:** four varnas – brahmin, kshatriya, vaishya and shudra

Chitpavan: a brahmin community of Maharashtra

Dalitbahujan: an umbrella term used to collectively refer to the Scheduled Castes, Scheduled Tribes, Other Backward Classes and minorities such as Dalit Muslims, Dalit Christians, Dalit Sikhs and Dalit Buddhists. The term was coined by Kancha Ilaiah.

***Dasa*:** slave, servant or enemy

***Dasyus*:** slaves, demons; sometimes used interchangeably with dasa

Dharma: sacred duty, religion, righteousness

Dharma Shastra: Sanskrit texts which collectively refer to the Hindu tenets of dharma; there are between eighteen to a hundred Sanskrit texts, with different and conflicting opinions, which are part of the Hindu Dharma shastra.

Dravidians: speakers of any of the Dravidian languages. Dravidians account for the majority of the population in southern India. They are also natively found in Pakistan, Afghanistan, Nepal, the Maldives and Sri Lanka.

***Dwija*:** the twice-born; *see* Antyaja

Ezhava: a Dalit community in Kerala

Harijans: literally 'children of God/Hari'; originally coined by Narsinh Mehta, a Gujarati saint–poet from the fifteenth century, who used the term to describe the 'bastard' children born to Devadasis. Later, Gandhiji popularised this term by calling the 'untouchables' 'Harijans'.

Jainism: a religion believed to have been founded by Rishabhanatha, the first Tirthankara. It holds as its core principles non-violence and peace. Mahavira, also known as Vardhamāna, is the last tirthankara, and one of the most influential teachers and propagators of Jainism. Jainism has two main sects – Swetambara and Digambara.

Karana: a community of scribes in Odisha

Karma: action, work or deed. It also refers to the spiritual principle of cause and effect where the intent and actions of an individual influence his/her future.

Khandayat: a warrior community in Odisha

Kondh: a tribal community of Odisha

Mahar: a Dalit community of Maharashtra

Mahima Dharma: a religious sect started by Mahima Goswami in the middle of the nineteenth century in Odisha. The literal meaning of 'Mahima' is 'glory'. As believers of the nirguna tradition, followers of Mahima Dharma believe that God is *alekha* (about whom nothing has been written), *niranjana* (who has no attributes) and *nirakara* (formless). Bhima Bhoi, a tribal poet of Odisha, propagated this philosophy in a major way. A majority of its followers are Dalits and Adivasis.

Mala: a Dalit community of Andhra Pradesh

Mang: a Dalit community of Maharashtra

***Manusmriti*:** an ancient Hindu legal text, attributed to Svayambhuva Manu

Neo-Buddhists: a term that is used to describe Ambedkar and his followers who converted to Buddhism in 1956

Nishada: an ancient tribal community; also the name of a tribal kingdom as described in the Mahabharata

Panchama: a member of the fifth and lowest caste; 'untouchables'

Panchasakhas: the five saint–poets from medieval Odisha: Balarama Dasa, Jagannatha Dasa, Achyutanada Dasa, Jasobanta Dasa and

Ananta Dasa. They were critical of orthodox caste practices in Odia society.

Pariah: outcaste, untouchable

Prakrit: used to refer to a number of Middle Indo-Aryan languages of which Ardhamagadhi Prakrit is supposed to be the definitive version. It was used by lower castes and women in ancient India as they were denied access to Sanskrit in any form.

Purana: literal meaning 'ancient'. It refers to a vast genre of Indian literature on a wide range of topics, particularly myths, legends and other traditional lore. Composed primarily in Sanskrit, but also in regional languages, there are as many as thirty-six volumes including the Upa (additional) puranas. Each purana has the name of a god or one of his incarnations. The titles of the main Puranas are: Brahma, Vishnu, Shiva, Garuda, Vayu, Agni, Skanda and Bhagavata.

Rakshasa: an evil spirit, a demon

Rig Veda: A collection of Vedic Sanskrit hymns, the Rig Veda is the first of the four Vedas, that is, canonical texts of Hindu mythology with the other three being the Sam, Yajur and Atharva Veda.

Samskara: rites relating to birth, marriage and death in Hinduism

Savara: a tribal community of Odisha

Siddha: the accomplished one; an ascetic who has achieved enlightenment

Smritis: Literally 'that which is remembered', the smritis are a body of Hindu texts usually attributed to an author, traditionally written down but constantly revised, in contrast to Vedic literature which was considered authorless, that were transmitted verbally across generations and fixed. Smriti is a derivative secondary work. The smriti literature is a corpus of diverse varied texts which include, but is not limited to, the epics (the *Mahabharata* and *Ramayana*), the Dharmasutras and Dharma shastras, the Arthasastras and the puranas. Each smriti text exists in many versions, with many different readings.

Sutras: an aphorism or other teaching that is part of Hinduism, Buddhism and Jainism

Upanishads: a part of the Vedas, Upanishads are ancient Sanskrit texts that contain some of the central philosophical concepts and ideas of Hinduism, some of which are shared with Buddhism, Jainism and Sikhism.

Varkaris: a Marathi term for pilgrims; specifically applied to those who make the journey to Pandharpur or who are devotees of Vitthoba

Varna: 'type', 'order', 'colour' or 'class'; it is often used to denote the four castes of Hinduism

Vedanta: literally 'end of the Vedas'. Also known as the Uttara Mimamsa, it is one of the six orthodox schools of Indian philosophy.

Suggested Reading

PRIMARY SOURCES

Anand, Mulk Raj. *Untouchable*. New Delhi: Arnold Associates, 1981, 1935. Print.

Anand, Mulk Raj, and Eleanor Zelliot, eds. *An Anthology of Dalit Literature: Poems*. New Delhi: Gyan, 1992. Print.

Bagul, Baburao. *When I Hid My Caste: Stories*. Trans. Jerry Pinto. New Delhi: Speaking Tiger, 2018. Print.

Bama. *Harum-Scarum Saar and Other Stories*. Trans. N. Ravi Shankar. New Delhi: Women Unlimited, 2006. Print.

---. *Karukku*. Trans. Lakshmi Holmström. Chennai: Macmillan, 2000. Print.

---. *Sangati*. Trans. Lakshmi Holmström. New Delhi: Oxford UP, 2009. Print.

---. *Vanmam: Vendetta*. Trans. Malini Seshadri. New Delhi: Oxford UP, 2008. Print.

Basu, Romen. *Outcast.* New Delhi: Sterling Publishers, 1986. Print.

Basu, Tapan, A. Mangai, and Indranil Acharya, eds. *Listen to the Flames*. New Delhi: Oxford UP, 2016. Print.

Bhave, Sumitra. *Pan on Fire*. Trans. Gauri Deshpande. New Delhi: Indian Social Institute, 1988. Print.

Biswas, Manohar Mouli. *Surviving in My World: Growing up Dalit in Bengal*. Trans. Jaideep Sarangi and Angana Dutta. Kolkata: Samya, 2015. Print.

Burke, Rupalee, and Darshana Trivedi, trans. and ed. *The Silver Lining: Gujarati Dalit Poetry*. Ahmedabad: Gujarat Dalit Sahitya Akademi, 2000. Print.

---. *Tongues of Fire: A Selection of Gujarati Dalit Short Stories*. Ahmedabad: Gujarat Dalit Sahitya Akademi, 2000. Print.

Byapari, Manoranjan. *Interrogating My Chandal Life: An Autobiography of a Dalit*. Trans. Sipra Mukherjee. New Delhi: Sage-Samya, 2018. Print.

Chokhamela. *On the Threshold: Songs of Chokhamela*. Trans. Rohini Mokashi-Punekar. New Delhi: The Book Review Literary Trust, 2002. Print.

Dangle, Arjun, ed. *A Corpse in the Well: Translations from Modern Marathi Dalit Autobiographies*. Hyderabad: Disha Books, 1994. Print.

---, ed. *No Entry for the New Sun: Translations from Modern Marathi Dalit Poetry*. Hyderabad: Sangam Books, 1992. Print.

---, ed. *Poisoned Bread: Translations from Modern Marathi Dalit Literature*. Bombay: Orient Longman, 1992. Print.

Das, D. P. *The Untouchable Story*. Delhi: Allied Publishers, 1985. Print.

Dasan, M., V. Pratibha, C. S. Chandrika, and Pradeepan. P., eds. *The Oxford India Anthology of Malayalam Dalit Writing*. New Delhi: Oxford UP, 2012. Print.

Dharman, Cho. *Koogai: The Owl*. Trans. Vasantha Surya. New Delhi: Oxford UP, 2015. Print.

Dhasal, Namdeo. *Namdeo Dhasal: Poet of the Underworld, Poems 1972–2006*. Trans. Dilip Chitre. New Delhi: Navayana, 2007. Print.

Freeman, James M. *Untouchable: An Indian Life History*. London: George Allen and Unwin, 1979. Print.

Gadhvi, Praveen. *The City of Dust and Lust*. Trans. Praveen Gadhvi. Delhi: B. S. Publishers, 2010. Print.

Gaikwad, Laxman. *The Branded*. Trans. P. A. Kolharkar. New Delhi: Sahitya Akademi, 1998. Print.

Gajvee, Premanand. *The Strength of Our Wrists: Three Plays*. Trans. Shanta Gokhale and M. D. Hatkanangalekar. New Delhi: Navayana, 2013. Print.

Gidla, Sujatha. *Ants among Elephants: An Untouchable Family and the Making of Modern India*. Noida: Harper Collins, 2017. Print.

Goswami, Bonomali. *Untouchables: A Novel*. New Delhi: Mittal Publications, 1994. Print.

Gunasekharan, K. A. *The Scar*. Trans. V. Kadambari. Chennai: Orient BlackSwan, 2009. Print.

Hazari. *Untouchable: The Autobiography of an Indian Outcaste*. New York: Pralger Publishers, 1970. Print.

Jadhav, Narendra. *Outcaste: A Memoir*. New Delhi: Viking, 2003. Print.

Jashuva, Gurram. *Bat*. Trans. K. Madhava Rao. Hyderabad: Jashuva Foundation, 1998. Print.

Jatav, D. R. *A Silent Soldier: An Autobiography*. Jaipur: Samata Sahitya Sadan, 2000. Print.

Kale, Kishore Shantabai. *Against All Odds*. Trans. Sandhya Pandey. New Delhi: Penguin, 2000. Print.

Kalidasa. *The Abhijñānashākuntalam of Kalidasa*. Trans. M. R. Kale. Delhi: Motilal Banarsidas, 2010. Print.

Kalyan Rao, G. *Untouchable Spring*. Trans. Alladi Uma and M. Sridhar. New Delhi: Orient BlackSwan, 2010. Print.

Kamble, Baby. *The Prisons We Broke*. Trans. Maya Pandit. New Delhi: Orient BlackSwan, 2011. Print.

Kandasamy, Meena. *Miss Militancy*. New Delhi: Navayana, 2012. Print.

---. *The Gypsy Goddess: a Mighty Thunderclap of a Novel*. New Delhi: Fourth Estate, 2014. Print.

---. *When I Hit You Or, a Portrait of the Writer as a Young Wife*. New Delhi: Juggernaut, 2017. Print.

Kesharshivam, B. *The Whole Truth and Nothing but the Truth: A Dalit's Life*. Trans. Gita Chaudhuri. Kolkata: Samya, 2008. Print.

Lakshminarayana, Unnava. *Malapalli*. Trans. V. V. B. Rama Rao. New Delhi: Sahitya Akademi, 2008. Print.

Limbale, Sharankumar. *Hindu: A Novel*. Trans. Arun Prabha Mukherjee. Kolkata: Samya, 2010. Print.

---. *The Dalit Brahmin and Other Stories*. Trans. Priya Adarkar. Hyderabad: Orient BlackSwan, 2018. Print.

---. *The Outcaste*. Trans. Santosh Bhoomkar. New Delhi: Oxford UP, 2003. Print.

Macwan, Joseph. *The Stepchild*. Trans. Rita Kothari. New Delhi: Oxford UP, 2004. Print.

Madhopuri, Balbir. *Changiya Rukh: Against the Night: An Autobiography*. Trans. Tripti Jain. New Delhi: Oxford UP, 2010. Print.

Mahadeva, Devanoora. *Kusumabale*. New Delhi: Oxford UP, 2015. Print.

Malagatti, Aravind. *Government Brahmana*. Trans. Dharani Devi Malagatti, Janet Vucinich and N. Subramanya. Chennai: Orient Longman, 2007. Print.

Mane, Laxman. *Outsider*. Trans. A. K. Kamat. New Delhi: Sahitya Akademi, 1997. Print.

Mangalam, Harish. *Light of Darkness: Gujarati Short Stories*. Trans. Rupalee Burke. Delhi: Yash Publications, 2012. Print.

Mangalam, Harish, and M. B. Gaijan. *Pristine Land: Gujarati Dalit Literature*. Delhi: Yash Publications, 2009.

Moon, Vasant. *Vasti: Growing up Untouchable in India: A Dalit Autobiography*. Trans. Gail Omvedt. USA: Rowman and Littlefield Publishers, 2001. Print.

Naik, Akhila. *Bheda*. Trans. Raj Kumar. New Delhi: Oxford UP, 2017. Print.

Navaria, Ajay. *Unclaimed Terrain*. Trans. Laura Brueck. New Delhi: Navayana, 2013. Print.

Pawar, Daya. *Baluta*. Trans. Jerry Pinto. New Delhi: Speaking Tiger, 2015. Print.

Pawar, Urmila. *Mother Wit*. Trans. Veena Deo. New Delhi: Zubaan, 2013. Print.

---. *The Weave of My Life: A Dalit Woman's Memoirs*. Trans. Maya Pandit. New York: Columbia UP, 2009. Print.

Pawar, Urmila, and Meenakshi Moon. *We Also Made History: Women in the Ambedkarite Movement*. New Delhi: Zubaan, 2008. Print.

Purushottam, K., Gita Ramaswamy, and Gogu Syamala, eds. *The Oxford India Anthology of Telugu Dalit Writing*. New Delhi: Oxford UP, 2016. Print.

Racine, Josiane, and Jean-Luc. *Viramma: Life of an Untouchable*. Trans. Will Hobson. Paris: Verso, 1997. Print.

Rajkumar, N. D. *Give Us This Day a Feast of Flesh*. Trans. Anushiya Ramaswamy. New Delhi: Navayana, 2010. Print.

Ravikumar, and R. Azhagarasan, eds. *The Oxford India Anthology of Tamil Dalit Writing*. New Delhi: Oxford UP, 2012. Print.

Satyanarayana, K., and Susie Tharu, eds. *No Alphabet in Sight: New Dalit Writing from South India*. Dossier 1. Tamil and Malayalam. New Delhi: Penguin Books, 2011. Print.

---, ed. *Steel Nibs Are Sprouting: New Dalit Writing from South India*. Dossier 2. Telugu and Kannada. New Delhi: Penguin Books, 2013. Print.

Shyamala, Gogu. *Father May be an Elephant and Mother only a Small Basket, But* . . . . New Delhi: Navayana, 2012. Print.

Shyamlal. *Untold Story of a Bhangi Vice-Chancellor*. Jaipur: University Book House, 2001. Print.

Siddalingaiah. *A Word with You, World: The Autobiography of a Poet*. Trans. S. R. Ramakrishna. New Delhi: Navayana, 2013. Print.

Singh, Balwant. *An Untouchable in the IAS*. Saharanpur: Prem Printing Press, 1997. Print.

Singha, Sankar Prasad, and Indranil Acharya. *Survival and Other Stories: Bangla Dalit Fiction in Translation*. New Delhi: Orient BlackSwan, 2012. Print.

Sivakami, P. *The Grip of Change*. Trans. P. Sivakami. Chennai: Orient Longman, 2006. Print.

---. *The Taming of Women*. Trans. Pritham K. Chakravarty. New Delhi: Penguin, 2012. Print.

Sunani, Basudev. *Cast Out: Poems of Anger and Angst*. Trans. J. P. Das. Bhubaneswar: Rupantar, 2008. Print.

Valmiki, Omprakash. *Amma and Other Stories*. Trans. Naresh K. Jain. New Delhi: Manohar, 2008. Print.

---. *Joothan: A Dalit's Life*. Trans. Arun Prabha Mukherjee. Kolkata: Samya, 2007. Print.

SECONDARY SOURCES

Abraham, Joshil K., and Judith Misrahi-Barak, eds. *Dalit Literatures in India*. New Delhi: Routledge, 2016. Print.

Ahmad, Imtiaz, and Shashi Bhushan Upadhyay. *Dalit Assertion in Society, Literature and History*. Delhi: Deshkal Publication, 2007. Print.

Ambedkar, B. R. *The Untouchables: Who Were They and Why They Became Untouchables*. Bombay: The Education Department, Government of Maharashtra, 1990. Print.

---. *What Congress and Gandhi have Done for Untouchables*. Bombay: Thacker and Co, 1945. Print.

Anandhi, S., and Karin Kapadia, eds. *Dalit Women: Vanguard of an Alternative Politics in India*. London: Routledge, 2017. Print.

Anand, S. *Touchable Tales: Publishing and Reading Dalit Literature*. Chennai: Navayana, 2007. Print.

Chatterjee, Angana. *Violent Gods: Hindu Nationalism in India's Present, Narratives from Orissa*. Gurgaon: Three Essays Collective, 2010. Print.

Arnold, David, and Blackburn Stuart, ed. *Telling Lives in India: Biography, Autobiography and Life History*. Bloomington: Indiana UP, 2004. Print.

Aryama, and Sukhadeo Thorat. *Ambedkar in Retrospect: Essays on Economics, Politics and Society*. New Delhi: Rawat Publications, 2007. Print.

Aston, N. M. *Literature of Marginality: Dalit Literature and African American Literature*. New Delhi: Prestige Books, 2001. Print.

Baghel, Indu. *Dalit Women's Movement in Modern India*. New Delhi: Jnanada Prakashan, 2009. Print.

Banerjee-Dube, Ishita, ed. *Caste in History*. New Delhi: Oxford UP, 2010. Print.

Basu, Swaraj. *Readings on Dalit Identity: History, Literature and Religion*. New Delhi: Orient BlackSwan, 2016. Print.

Basu, Tapan, ed. *Translating Caste*. New Delhi: Katha, 2002. Print.

Bhagavan, Manu, and Anne Feldhaus, ed. *Claiming Power from Below: Dalits and Subaltern Question in India*. New Delhi: Oxford UP, 2011. Print.

---, ed. *Speaking Truth to Power: Religion, Caste, and the Subaltern Question in India*. New Delhi: Oxford UP, 2009. Print.

Bharathi, Thummapudi. *A History of Telugu Dalit Literature*. New Delhi: Kalpaz, 2008. Print.

Bhattacharya, Sabyasachi, and Yagati Chinna Rao, ed. *The Past of the Outcaste: Readings in Dalit History*. Hyderabad: Orient BlackSwan, 2017. Print.

Brodov, V. *Indian Philosophy in Modern Times*. Moscow: Progressive Publisher, 1984. Print.

Brueck, Laura R. *Writing Resistance: The Rhetorical Imagination of Hindi Literature*. New York: Columbia UP, 2014. Print.

Chakravarti, Uma. *Gendering Caste: Through a Feminist Lens*. Calcutta: Stree, 2003. Print.

Chalam, K. S. *Modernization and Dalit Education: Ambedkar's Vision*. New Delhi: Rawat Publications, 2008. Print.

Chattopadhyaya, D. P. *Lokayata: A Study of Ancient Indian Materialism*. Delhi: People's Publishing House, 1992. Print.

Chitre, Dilip. 'The Architecture of Anger: On Namdeo Dhasal's "Golpitha"'. *Journal of South Asian Literature* 17.1 (Winter–Spring 1982): 93–95. Print.

Clark, T. W. *The Novel in India: Its Birth and Development*. London: George Allen and Unwin, 1970. Print.

Dahiwale, S. M, ed. *Understanding Indian Society: The Non-Brahmanic Perspective*. Jaipur: Rawat Publications, 2005. Print.

Das, Sisir Kumar. 'The Narrative of Suffering: Caste and the Underprivileged'. *Translating Caste*. Ed. Tapan Basu. New Delhi: Katha, 2002. Print.

Dasan, M., and Rajesh Karankal, eds. *Counter Cultural Discourse and Dalit Literature in India*. New Delhi: ABD Publishers, 2014. Print.

Deliege, Robert. *The World of the 'Untouchables': Paraiyars of Tamil Nadu*. New Delhi: Oxford UP, 1997. Print.

Deshpande, G. P., ed. *Selected Writings of Jotirao Phule*. New Delhi: Left Word, 2002. Print.

Devi, Vidya. *Dalit and Social Justice*. New Delhi: MD Publications, 2008. Print.

Dirks, Nicholas B. *Castes of Mind: Colonialism and the Making of Modern India*. New Delhi: Permanent Black, 2001. Print.

Duggal, K. S., ed. *Writer in Freedom Struggle*. Chandigarh: Twenty-first Century Indian Society, 1988. Print.

Dussel, Enrique. *Philosophy of Liberation*. Trans. Aquilina Martinez and Christine Morkovsky. New York: Orbis, 1985. Print.

Deo, Fanindam. *Roots of Poverty: A Social History*. Bhubaneswar: Amadeus Press, 2009. Print.

Felski, Rita. *Uses of Literature*. Blackwell: United Kingdom, 2008. Print.

Fischer, Ernst. *The Necessity of Art: A Marxist Approach*. London: Verso Reprint, 2010. Print.

Fleishman, Avrom. *Fiction and the Ways of Knowing*. Austin: U of Texas P, 1978. Print.

Forrester, Duncan B. *Caste and Christianity*. London: Clarion Press, 1980. Print.

Foucault, Michael. *Power/Knowledge*. Ed. Paul Rabinow. New York: Peregrine Books, 1984. Print.

Franco, Fernando, et al. *Journeys to Freedom: Dalit Narratives*. Kolkata: Samya, 2004. Print.

Gajarawala, Toral Jatin. *Untouchable Fictions: Literary Realism and the Crisis of Caste*. New York: Fordham UP, 2013. Print.

Galanter, Marc. *Competing Equalities.* Delhi: Oxford UP, 1994. Print.

Gandhi, M. K. *Collected Works of Mahatma Gandhi.* Volume XIX. Delhi: The Publications Division, Ministry of Information and Broadcasting, Government of India, 1966. Print.

Ganguly, Debjani. *Caste and Dalit Lifeworlds: Postcolonial Perspectives*. New Delhi: Orient BlackSwan, 2008. Print.

---. *Caste, Colonialism and Counter-modernity: Notes on a Postcolonial Hermeneutics of Caste*. New York and London: Routledge, 2005. Print.

Ghose, Shankar. *The Western Impact on Indian Politics*. New Delhi: Allied Publishers, 1967. Print.

Ghurye, G. S. *Caste and Race in India*. Mumbai: Popular Prakashan, 2008. Print.

Gore, M. S. *The Social Context of an Ideology: Ambedkar's Political and Social Thought*. New Delhi: Sage, 1994. Print.

Gorringe, Hugo. *Untouchable Citizens: Dalit Movement and Democratisation in Tamil Nadu*. New Delhi: Sage Publications, 2005. Print.

Gould, Harold A. *The Hindu Caste System*. Delhi: Chanakya Publications, 1987. Print.

Gupta, Charu. *The Gender of Caste: Representing Dalits in Print*. Ranikhet: Permanent Black, 2016. Print.

Guru, Gopal. *Dalit Cultural Movement and Dialectics of Dalit Politics in Maharashtra*. Mumbai: Vikas Adhyayan Kendra, 1997. Print.

---, ed. *Humiliation: Claims and Context*. New Delhi: Oxford UP, 2009. Print.

Guru, Gopal, and Sundar Sarukkai. *The Cracked Mirror: An Indian Debate on Experience and Theory*. New Delhi: Oxford UP, 2012. Print.

Hardtmann, Eva-Mari. *The Dalit Movement in India: Local Practices, Global Connections*. New Delhi: Oxford UP, 2010. Print.

Hunt, Sarah Beth. *Hindi Dalit Literature and the Politics of Representation*. New Delhi: Routledge, 2014. Print.

Ilaiah, Kancha. *Buffalo Nationalism: A Critique of Spiritual Fascism*. Kolkata: Samya, 2007. Print.

---. *God as Political Philosopher: Buddha's Challenge to Brahmanism*. Calcutta: Samya, 2001. Print.

---. *Post-Hindu India: A Discourse on Dalit-Bahujan Socio-Spiritual and Scientific Revolution*. New Delhi: Sage, 2009. Print.

---. *The Weapon of the Other: Dalit Bahujan Writings and the Remaking of Nationalist Thought*. New Delhi: Pearson, 2010. Print.

---. *Why I am Not a Hindu: A Sudra Critique of Hindutva Philosophy, Culture and Political Economy*. Calcutta: Samya, 1996. Print.

Irudayam, Aloysius, S. J., et al. *Dalit Women Speak Out: Caste, Class and Gender Violence in India*. New Delhi: Zubaan, 2014. Print.

Jadhav, P. B. *Dalits and Human Rights: Emerging Scenario*. Jaipur: Vital Publications, 2010. Print.

Jaffrelot, Christophe. *Dr Ambedkar and Untouchability: Analysing and Fighting Caste*. New Delhi: Permanent Black, 2006. Print.

Jiloha, R. C. *The Native Indian: In Search of Identity*. New Delhi: Blumoon Books, 1995. Print.

Jogdand, P.G, ed. *Dalit Women: Issues and Perspectives*. New Delhi: Gyan Publishing House, 1995. Print.

Joshi, Barbara, ed. *Untouchable: Voices of the Dalit Liberation Movement*. New Delhi: Select Book Service Syndicate, 1986. Print.

Joshi, Svati, ed. *Re-Thinking English*. New Delhi: Trianka, 1991. Print.

Keer, Dhananjay. *Mahatma Jotirao Phule: Father of Indian Social Revolution*. Bombay: Papular Prakashan, 2000. Print.

Khandekar, Tarachand. 'Literature of Revolt and Resurgence'. *The First All India Dalit Writers Conference: A Commemorative Volume*. Ed. Bojja

Tharakam. Hyderabad: Dr B. R. Ambedkar Memorial Trust, 1994. Print

Knappert, Jan. *Indian Mythology*. London: Diamond Books, 1995. Print.

Kosambi, D. D. *The Culture and Civilisation of Ancient India in Historical Outline*. Delhi: Vikas, 1965. Print.

Kothari, Rita. *Translating India*. New Delhi: Cambridge UP, 2006. Print.

Kshirsagar, R.K. *Dalit Movement in India and Its Leaders*. New Delhi: Prints India, 1994. Print.

Kumar, Akshaya. *Poetry, Politics and Culture: Indian Texts and Contexts*. Routledge: Delhi, 2009. Print.

Kumar, Arun, and Sanjay Kumar, ed. *Dalit Studies in Higher Education: Vision and Challenges*. Deshkal: Delhi, 2005. Print.

Kumar, Raj. 'Caste and the Literary Imagination in the Context of Odia Literature: A Reading of Akhila Naik's *Bheda*'. *Dalit Literatures in India.* Ed. Judith Misrahi-Barak and Joshil. K. Abraham. New Delhi: Routledge, 2016. Print.

---. *Dalit Personal Narratives: Reading Caste, Nation and Identity*. New Delhi: Orient BlackSwan, 2010. Print.

---. Translator's Note. *Bheda*. By Akhila Naik. Trans. Raj Kumar. New Delhi: Oxford UP, 2017. Print.

Kumar, Vivek. *Caste and Democracy in India: A Perspective from Below*. New Delhi: Gyan Publishing House, 2014. Print.

Kunhappa, Murkot. *Sree Narayana Guru*. Delhi: National Book Trust, 1988. Print.

Limbale, Sharankumar. *Towards an Aesthetic of Dalit Literature: History, Controversies and Considerations.* Trans. Alok Mukherjee. New Delhi: Orient Longman, 2004. Print.

Mani, Braj Ranjan. *Debrahmanising History: Dominance and Resistance in Indian History*. Delhi: Manohar, 2005. Print.

---. *Knowledge and Power: A Discourse for Transformation*. Delhi: Manohar, 2014. Print.

Massey, James. *Dalit Theology: History, Context, Text and Whole Salvation*. New Delhi: Manohar, 2014. Print.

Mines, Mattison. 'Social Stratification among Muslim Tamils in Tamil Nadu, South India'. *Caste and Social Stratification among Muslims in India*. Ed. Imtiaz Ahmad. New Delhi: Manohar, 1978. 159–70. Print.

Modi, S. K. *Dalits: A Low Caste of Hinduism*. New Delhi: Navyug, 2008. Print.

Ganesh, Mogalli. *Dalitaru mattu jagatikarana*. Trans. Rajendra Chenni. Hampi: Kannada University, 1998. Translated and quoted in 'Struggles over the Sign: Discourses on English' by Rajendra Chenni and included in Uma, Alladi et al., ed. *English in the Dalit Context*. New Delhi: Orient BlackSwan, 2014.

Moon, Vasant. *Dr Babasaheb Ambedkar: Writings and Speeches*. Volumes 1 to 18. Bombay: Education Department, Government of Maharashtra, 1989. Print.

Morris, Rosalind C., ed. *Can the Subaltern Speak?: Reflections on the History of an Idea*. New York: Columbia UP, 2010. Print.

Mukherjee, Alok. *The Gift of English: English Education and the Formation of Alternative Hegemonies in India*. New Delhi: Orient BlackSwan, 2009. Print.

Mukherjee, Meenakshi, ed. *Early Novels in India*. New Delhi: Sahitya Akademi, 2010. Print.

---. 'English in an Uneven Land, English in an Uneven World: Literature in English Translation'. *Southern Postcolonialisms: The Global South and the 'New' Literary Representations*. Ed. Sumanyu Satpathy. New Delhi: Routledge, 2009. 17–29. Print.

Mukherjee, Prabhati. *Beyond the Four Varnas: The Untouchables in India*. Shimla: Indian Institute of Advanced Study, 1988. Print.

Murthy, B. S. *Depressed and Oppressed*. New Delhi: S. Chand and Co, 1971. Print.

Nagaraj, D. R. *The Flaming Feet and Other Essays: The Dalit Movement in India*. Ranikhet: Permanent Black, 2010. Print.

Namishray, Mohan Dass. *Caste and Race: Comparative Study of B.R. Ambedkar and Martin Luther King*. Jaipur: Rawat Publications, 2003. Print.

---. *Dalit Freedom Fighters*. New Delhi: Gyan Publications, 2010. Print.

Narayan, Badri. *Documenting Dissent: Contesting Fables, Contested Memories and Dalit Political Discourse*. Shimla: Indian Institute of Advanced Study, 2001. Print.

---. *The Making of the Dalit Public in North India: Uttar Pradesh, 1950–Present*. New Delhi: Oxford UP, 2011.

---. *Women Heroes and Dalit Assertion in North India: Identity, Culture and Politics*. New Delhi: Sage Publications, 2006. Print.

Narayan, Badri, and Mishra, A. R, ed. *Multiple Marginalities: An Anthology of Identified Dalit Writings*. New Delhi: Manohar, 2004. Print.

Nirmal, Arvind P. *Heuristic Explorations*. Madras: CLS, 1990. Print.

O'Hanlon, Rosalind. *Caste, Conflict and Ideology: Mahatma Jotirao Phule and Low Caste Protest in Nineteenth-century Western India*. Cambridge: Cambridge UP, 1985. Print.

Olsen, S. H. 'Literary Aesthetics and Literary Practice'. *Mind* 90 (1981): 533. Print.

Omvedt, Gail. 'A Proposal for Dalit Studies'. *Dalit Studies in Higher Education: Vision and Challenges*. Ed. Arun Kumar and Sanjay Kumar. New Delhi: Deshkal, 2005. 17–25. Print.

---. *Ambedkar: Towards an Enlightened India*. New Delhi: Penguin, 2004. Print.

---. *Buddhism in India: Challenging Brahmanism and Caste*. New Delhi: Sage Publications, 2003. Print.

---. *Cultural Revolt in Colonial Society: The Non-Brahman Movement in Western India, 1873 to 1930*. Bombay: Scientific Socialist Education Trust, 1976. Print.

---. *Dalits and the Democratic Revolution: Dr Ambedkar and the Dalit Movement in Colonial India*. New Delhi: Sage Publications, 1994. Print.

---. *Dalit Visions*. Hyderabad: Orient BlackSwan, 2006. Print.

---. *Understanding Caste: From Buddha to Ambedkar and Beyond*. New Delhi: Orient BlackSwan, 2011. Print.

Pandey, Gyanendra. *Routine Violence: Race, Caste, and Difference in India and the United States*. New Delhi: Cambridge UP, 2013. Print.

Pandian, M. S. S. *Brahmin and Non-Brahmin: Genealogies of the Tamil Political Present*. Ranikhet: Permanent Black, 2007. Print.

Phule, Jotiba. *Collected Works of Mahatma Jotirao Phule.* Volumes I and II. Translated by P.G. Patil. Bombay: Education Department, Government of Maharashtra, 1991. Print.

Pradhan, Prasant Kumar. *Beginning a Dalit Discourse in Odisha: Scheduled Caste Identity in the 20th Century*. Cuttack: A. K. Mishra Publishers, 2016. Print.

Prakash, Aseem. *Dalit Capital: State, Markets and Civil Society in Urban India*. New Delhi: Routledge, 2015. Print.

Prasad, Amar Nath, and M. B. Gaijan, ed. *Dalit Literature: A Critical Exploration*. New Delhi: Sarup and Sons, 2010. Print.

Prasad, Chandra Bhan. 'Reinventing Lord Macaulay'. *Countercurrents*, 27 October 2004. www.countercurrents.org/dalit-prasad271004.htm. Accessed 20 May 2018.

Prashad, Vijay. *Untouchable Freedom: A Social History of a Dalit Community*. New Delhi: Oxford UP, 2001. Print.

Rajan, Rajeshwari Sunder. *The Lie of the Land*. New Delhi: Oxford UP, 1992. Print.

Rajkumar, Peniel. *Dalit Theology and Dalit Liberation: Problems, Paradigms and Possibilities*. England: Ashgate, 2010. Print.

Ram, Jagjivan. *Caste Challenge in India*. New Delhi: Vision Books, 1980. Print.

Ramakrishnan, E. V. *Making It New: Modernism in Malayalam, Marathi and Hindi Poetry*. Shimla: Indian Institute of Advanced Study, 1995. Print.

Rani, K. Suneetha. 'Does Translation Empower a Dalit Text?'. *Language Forum* 33.1 (2007): 55–64. Print.

Rao, Anupama, ed. *Gender and Caste*. New Delhi: Kali for Women, 2005. Print.

---. *The Caste Question: Dalits and the Politics of Modern India*. New Delhi: Permanent Black, 2009. Print.

Rao, Yagati Chinna. *Dividing Dalits: Writing on Sub-Categorisation of Scheduled Castes*. New Delhi: Rawat Publication, 2009. Print.

Ravidas, Ajay. *Ambedkar and the Dalit Movement*. Jaipur: ABD Publishers, 2010. Print.

Ravikumar. *Venomous Touch: Notes on Caste, Culture and Politics*. Trans. R. Azhagarasan. Kolkata: Samya, 2007. Print.

Rawat, Ramnarayan S., and K. Satyanarayana, ed. *Dalit Studies*. Ranikhet: Permanent Black, 2016. Print.

Rege, Sharmila. *Against the Madness of Manu: B. R. Ambedkar's Writings on Brahmanical Patriarchy*. New Delhi: Navayana, 2013. Print.

---. *Writing Caste/Writing Gender: Reading Dalit Women Testimonies*. New Delhi: Zubaan, 2006. Print.

Riemenschneider, Dieter. 'The New English Language Literatures and the Globalization of Tertiary Education'. *Southern Postcolonialisms: The Global South and the 'New' Literary Representations*. Ed. Sumanyu Satpathy. New Delhi: Routledge, 2009. 97–110. Print.

Rodrigues, Valerian, ed. *The Essential Writings of B.R. Ambedkar*. New Delhi: Oxford UP, 2002. Print.

Sadangi, H. C., ed. *Emancipation of Dalits and the Freedom Struggle*. New Delhi: Isha Books, 2008. Print.

Satpathy, Sumanyu, ed. *Southern Postcolonialisms: The Global South and the 'New' Literary Representations*. Routledge: New Delhi, 2009. Print.

Satyanarayana, K., and Susie Tharu. *The Exercise of Freedom: An Introduction to Dalit Writing*. New Delhi: Navayana, 2013. Print.

Sharma, Pradeep K. *Dalit Politics and Literature*. New Delhi: Shipra, 2006. Print.

Shyamlal. *Untouchable Castes in India: The Raigar Movement (1940–2004)*. Jaipur: Rawat Publications, 2010. Print.

Singha, Sankar Prasad, and Indranil Acharya. *Towards Social Change: Essays on Dalit Literature*. New Delhi: Orient BlackSwan, 2014. Print.

Spivak, Gayatri Chakravorty. 'A Moral Dilemma'. *Can the Subaltern Speak?: Reflections on the History of an Idea*. Ed. Rosalind C. Morris. New York: Columbia UP, 2010. 21–78. Print.

Sreenivasan, S. 'Why Does Dalit Literature Matter?'. *Beyond Borders* 6:1–2 (2010): 24–28. Print.

Still, Clarinda. *Dalit Women: Honour and Patriarchy in South India*. New Delhi: Social Science Press, 2014. Print.

Tagore, Rabindranath. *Rabindra Rachanabali*. Volume VI, 125th Anniversary Edition. Santiniketan: Visva Bharati, 1986. Print.

Teltumbde, Anand. *Dalits: Past, Present and Future*. London and New York: Routledge, 2017. Print.

---. *Republic of Caste: Thinking Equality in the Time of Neoliberal Hindutva*. New Delhi: Navayana, 2018. Print.

---, ed. *Hindutva and Dalits: Perspectives for Understanding Communal Praxis*. Kolkata: Samya, 2005. Print.

Tharakam, Bojja, ed. *First All India Dalit Writers Conference: A Commemorative Volume*. Hyderabad: Dr B. R. Ambedkar Memorial Trust, 1994. Print.

Tharu, Susie, ed. *Subject to Change: Teaching Literature in the Nineties*. Orient Longman: Hyderabad, 1998. Print.

Theertha, Swami Dharma. *History of Hindu Imperialism*. Madras: Dalit Educational Literature Centre, 1941, 1992. Print.

Uma, Alladi, et al, eds. *English in the Dalit Context*. New Delhi: Orient BlackSwan, 2014. Print.

Umakant, and Sukhadeo Thorat, eds. *Caste, Race and Discrimination: Discourses in International Context*. Jaipur: Rawat Publications, 2009. Print.

Valmiki, Omprakash. *Dalit saundarya shastra*. New Delhi: Radhakrishna, 2001. Print.

Vinayaraj, Y. T. *Dalit Theology after Continental Philosophy*. Switzerland: Palgrave Macmillan, 2016. Print.

Viswanathan, Gauri. *Masks of Conquest: Literary Study and British Rule in India*. New Delhi: Oxford UP, 1989. Print.

---. *Outside the Fold: Conversion, Modernity, and Belief*. New Delhi: Oxford UP, 1989. Print.

Wakankar, Milind. *Subalternity and Religion: The Prehistory of Dalit Empowerment in South Asia*. London: Routledge, 2010. Print.

Zelliot, Eleanor. *Ambedkar's World: The Making of Babasaheb and the Dalit Movement*. New Delhi: Navayana, 2016. Print.

---. *From Untouchable to Dalit: Essays on the Ambedkar Movement*. New Delhi: Manohar, 1992. Print.

Other books in the series

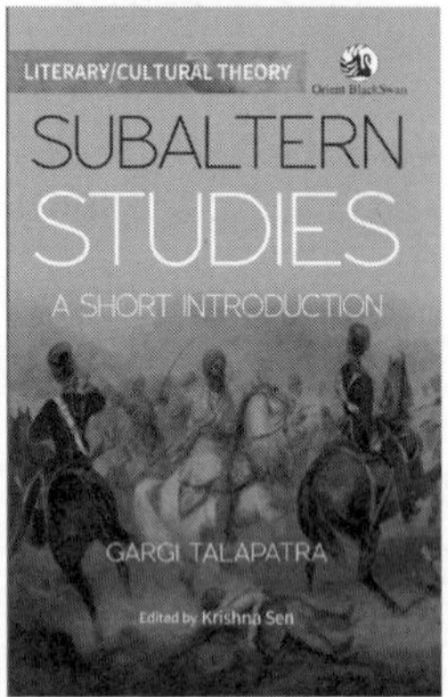

For more information, visit www.orientblackswan.com

Other books in the series

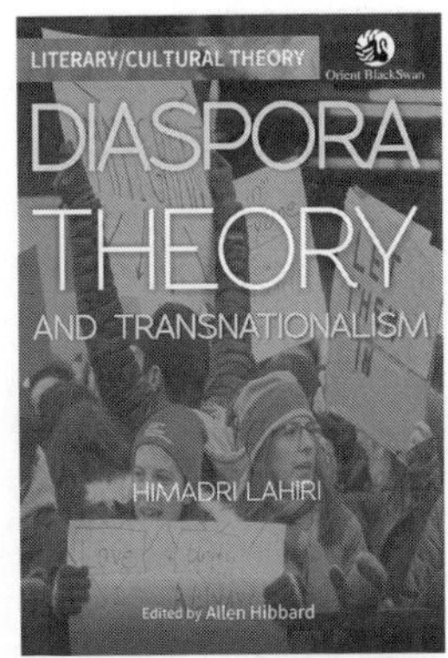

Other books in the series

For more information, visit www.orientblackswan.com